# MASTER THE ▲ART▼ OF TRADING
## AN INDISPENSABLE GUIDE TO INVESTING

**Lewis Daniels** is Chairman of Mayfair Ventures and has been trading from the age of fifteen, after visiting New York's Wall Street on a school trip from his native Wales. He has been educating and mentoring students in the Mayfair Method since 2012, teaching advanced techniques and introducing students to the professional side of trading. Daniels originally started writing *Master the Art of Trading* as a primer for his eleven-year-old son.

# MASTER THE ART OF TRADING

## AN INDISPENSABLE GUIDE TO INVESTING

### LEWIS DANIELS

HELIGO

Heligo
Books

Published in the UK by Heligo Books
An imprint of Bonnier Books UK
4th Floor, Victoria House
Bloomsbury Square
London, WC1B 4DA
England
Owned by Bonnier Books
Sveavägen 56, Stockholm, Sweden

Trade paperback – 978-1-788708-84-5
Ebook – 978-1-788708-85-2

A CIP catalogue of this book is available from the British Library.

Cover designed by Nick Stearn
Typeset by EnvyDesignLtd

Printed and bound in Great Britain by Clays Ltd, Elcograf S.p.A

1 3 5 7 9 10 8 6 4 2

Every reasonable effort has been made to trace copyright holders of
material reproduced in this book, but if any have been inadvertently
overlooked the publishers would be glad to hear from them.

Heligo Books is an imprint of Bonnier Books UK
www.bonnierbooks.co.uk

I want to thank my wife for her love and support in everything I do. I also want to dedicate the book to my son, Zack. This book was for him to learn to trade. Love you, Zack.

# CONTENTS

# FOREWORD

## BY PAUL VARCOE

When Lewis and I set up the Mayfair Method, I immediately realised that I would be the translator of the trading techniques that Lewis had developed. Here was obviously a great trading mind. The trick was to get the message across to other traders.

In this book, Lewis has simplified a lot of the techniques and lessons in an easy-to-follow format that I often translate in our daily streams.

The trouble with traders is that they are generally people with relatively high self-confidence and feelings of self-worth. These are laudable human traits in most situations, but they don't make for the best pupils. I'm like this myself, for goodness' sake. Very likely, so are you.

So, it's lucky you found this book.

Personally, I came from the trading world of derivatives.

'Why does that matter?' I hear you ask. It matters because for over 25 years, the trading I did didn't involve betting on market direction. I simply sold expensive options and bought cheap ones, and I generally didn't care if the market went up or down. So, I knew plenty about the stresses, strains and decisions of being a trader, about fundamentals and pricing and probability, but I had no real preconceptions when it came to learning how to pick market direction. I'd never really had to do it that much.

If you are an established trader, you probably do have these preconceptions and your own ideas, and the hardest part for you will be to take all your current opinions, tools and indicators and ignore them all. Again, if you are a complete novice, you have picked up the right book as this will take you from novice to pro.

If you haven't seen Lewis in action, you should definitely check out our Mayfair Method Discord server.

# INTRODUCTION

My name is Lewis Daniels, better known in the trading community as Mayfair Ventures, and co-founder of the Mayfair Method.

My trading journey started after a school trip to Wall Street. Looking back, this was a big deal, especially coming from Wales. My history teacher didn't want to teach anymore and was learning to trade as his route out. He had worked his magic and wangled a school trip as part of his lessons on the Wall Street Crash.

After seeing the pit – the sheer energy and freneticism of the trading floor – I knew it was something I wanted to do. On our return to Wales, the teacher came up with a challenge for the class. He'd picked up copies of the *Financial Times*, and all of us kids had to flip to the back pages that contained a double spread of stocks. The idea was simple: we had £10,000 of Monopoly money to invest in a stock just before Christmas 1999. In January, we would return and see who had earned the highest returns.

The rules were simple: you had to spend all the money, and you could pick any stock or as many stocks as you liked. The forms were then submitted to the teacher, who would do the workings-out and declare the winner in the first lesson back in the new year.

Some of my class bought things they liked; others spread themselves into 30 stocks. My strategy was, to me, more logical: I bought hi-tech stocks that I anticipated would grow over the Christmas period.

Well, I won!

And that's how I caught the trading bug – and I never looked back.

When I was 15, I would take my pushbike to the bank and get the branch manager to phone the broker to ask if the price was near the same as in the newspaper I would buy that day. I was buying yesterday's prices tomorrow.

A few years later, I got into penny stocks and the US stock market – think a wannabe *Wolf of Wall Street*. These stocks were bad. Although you could make a lot of money, they were similar to the crypto pump and dump plays in today's market.

As the internet became a factor, I found myself in the world of forex: the foreign exchange market, in which one currency is converted into another. It seemed even more exciting, and it didn't seem to shut like most nine-to-five stocks.

In 2012, I got suckered into one of these forex educational courses, where you pay a few thousand for little information. Boy, could they sell the dream – but they really didn't teach me anything I didn't already know.

# INTRODUCTION

It was on the back of these couple of days in London that I realised the issue with so-called financial gurus. They made more money from selling their courses than they actually did trading. With a friend from my local village, we decided to take the London business model into Wales.

The idea was simple: we would offer the base training for 80% less, localise it and allow people who never thought they could trade the opportunity to become traders! Teaching advanced techniques, in a simplified method. That has been my methodology ever since – and it's been incredibly effective. So effective, that I am now sharing this method with you now here, in *Master the Art of Trading*.

▼

I launched the Mayfair Method in early 2020. When the Covid-19 pandemic struck, I could not believe some of the rubbish I was seeing: the snake-oil salesman I had experienced in 2012 had moved into the digital space – YouTube videos, Instagram adverts, a course promising this, that and the other. It was scary.

During the first couple of months during the lockdowns in the UK, I digitalised some of my trading tools and built indicators for my online chart software.

Then I bumped into my old friend and former pit trader, Paul Varcoe. He was working at another forex education company and he was as alarmed as I was at all the false promises being peddled to unsuspecting new traders in the digital world. We decided to do something about it: something that would actually help novice traders to make it in this world.

And so the Mayfair Method was born in earnest – incorporating both our banks of knowledge and great expertise.

We wanted to help others who genuinely wanted to learn how to trade and not just buy signals or try to cut corners.

So far, the Mayfair Method has helped thousands of people gain the skills and confidence to trade, and from all walks of life – from doctors to lawyers, CEOs to entrepreneurs, pilots to plumbers – and from all around the world.

They have called the Mayfair Method a 'life-changing investment', 'the best money I ever spent', and have said 'I wish I'd found you earlier.' Many of our students have been struck by our accuracy in spotting trends and forecasting, with one messaging me: 'It pains me to admit it, but you are 100% right.' One of our subscribers has called Paul and me 'the joint GOAT' of the trading world.

The tools we teach has helped people make some serious money. These are the tools I will be teaching you in *Master the Art of Trading*.

# INTRODUCTION

gamble

/ˈgamb(ə)l/

verb

gerund or present participle: gambling

1. Play games of chance for money; bet.

*He gambles on football.*

Synonyms:
wager
place a bet
stake money on something
try one's luck
punt

2. Take risky action in the hope of a desired result.


trader

/ˈtreɪdə/

noun

plural: traders

A person who buys and sells goods, currency or shares.

Synonyms:
dealer
merchant
buyer
seller

## Chapter 1

# YOUR TRADING JOURNEY

When I started the Mayfair Method educational platform, it was to take trading education to the next level. Most commercial trading courses out there teach you how to competently place orders, plus some technical knowledge designed to give you the confidence to place those orders in the first place. Without this 'knowledge', only a fool would think they could walk into a casino that only returns 22–25% on average and come out on top. Why would anyone think they can win consistently with these types of odds?

In trading, there's a warning written on the home page of all of the brokers:

*CFDs are complex instruments and come with a high risk of losing money rapidly due to leverage. **73.18% of retail investor accounts lose money when trading CFDs with this provider**. You should consider whether you understand how CFDs* *work, and whether you can afford to take the high risk of losing your money.*

'Over 75% of traders lose money; you can lose more than you invest' is usually the general message.

So, think about it. The majority of educational courses available are part of the problem, and they are given by those who will likely profit from giving new traders the false confidence to go into the market and blow their accounts.

Usually, they even make you pay to take the course and then they recommend a broker to claim what's known as FTDs (First Time Deposits) from their affiliated broker.

Would you fly a plane after a one-month course if you knew your chances of survival were 25%? They give you just enough information for you to be dangerous to yourself.

What tickles me is that, in any professional sphere, people spend years training to become, for example, a lawyer or doctor, or any other profession. However, after watching a YouTube video or reading a tweet about an overnight Bitcoin billionaire, people think that with a small amount of money and some guidance from an influencer – hey presto, I'm on the way to riches.

What qualifies someone to be a trader? Most are just gamblers, totally clueless and hoping for a big break. Some people genuinely want to learn and understand more. The issue is, there is little trustworthy help out there or, worse, the complete opposite – many people just want signals and follow their influencers' every word.

Like any career or skill, you need to learn the fundamentals and practise.

As I often say, if you want to teach a man to fish, don't give him any fish.

I wanted to utilise my years of experience to help inform the online community and now the readers of this book. My intention was to create the 'university' course for those who had finished their school education – no hype, no get-rich-quick schemes, just sober analysis and well-thought-out money-making techniques.

It takes most people about a year to learn enough to be profitable. Few understand this and few have the patience required to trade in small amounts while they learn. This book will help you cut down the time required.

The idea is to show how traders can take a simplified journey into attaining the professional trading skills needed to make trading a success for them.

If you follow the Mayfair Method online, you will know we are not big on complicating things, we don't spend hours on streams we can deliver in ten minutes, and we don't use words where they are not needed. The same applies to this book.

Although I could probably write a full book on each of the individual chapters, I wanted to keep it simple and get the message across. With a little work and insight, you too can understand the complex world of trading.

When I tell students to read books by other authors on topics like Elliott Wave Theory or Wyckoff methods (don't worry if you don't know what they are, for now, as we will cover them later in this book), I often follow up with: 'Read it, absorb it and then throw 90% of it away.' Just keep the parts that matter to your trading style.

On your route to becoming a professional trader, I cannot emphasise enough that the real value is to strip it back.

Having more data or more analysis techniques doesn't necessarily lead to better investment decision-making. It often means more confusion and agony instead. Ever heard the expression 'I couldn't see the wood for all the trees?'

This book picks out the best aspects of each technique and plays down the rest. You end up with a refined version of all the best bits. That is the promise and the methodology of this book.

The trick is to simplify it.

I've spent a lot of time and a lot of money over the years trying to perfect my personal trading style – from going on courses to reading hundreds of books and taking thousands of trades – all in the pursuit of finding a more consistent trading method.

There is so much info out there, and you could spend your lifetime learning. So, I wanted to condense a lot of what I have gone through and share most of it in this book.

Whether you're new to trading or have been trading for years, I hope this book helps you on your trading journey.

'A HANDFUL OF MEN
HAVE BECOME VERY RICH
BY PAYING ATTENTION
TO DETAILS THAT MOST
OTHERS IGNORED.'

*HENRY FORD*

## Chapter 2

# UN-COMMON SENSE

'Un-common sense.'

It's a quote from my now-12-year-old son illustrating the difference between intelligence and common sense.

What do I mean by this? You might know a person who is clearly intelligent but at the same time exhibits little to no common sense. You come across these people in the trading world a lot; I often meet people who are viewed as the best in their professional fields, but who fail as traders.

For example, take a company director for a large blue-chip firm or a multi-millionaire tech start-up founder. They might be seen as highly successful in their fields; therefore, they assume they can be successful as traders. On paper, they have all the credentials: the focus, the drive, the mindset, the determination – perhaps an acumen for numbers. However, they fail as a result of their assumptions. Their misconceptions reveal *uncommon sense*.

Let's tackle a couple of these misconceptions.

Firstly, as professionals, they might have spent three to seven years earning their degree or PhD or other such qualifications. They might therefore feel that trading should be different. Why? Well, it's not. Trading takes time and experience and repetition to learn, and even longer to become a professional. Trading isn't a get-rich-quick scheme, and it shouldn't be viewed like one.

Another misconception is that you must have millions of dollars to play with in order to be a successful trader. If you have Trader A working for a large investment bank with a book size of £10 million a day, does this make them a good trader? I know such a trader and would question his 'ability' when he has four losing days in a row.

Then there's Trader B: a single mother with a £100 trading book, just trying to make a little extra money. Would you call them a bad trader if they only made 10% gains a month? Certainly not! To me, this is like calling out a doctor making £100,000 a year by saying that they are awful in their profession because they're not making £5 million a year working on Harley Street.

When it comes to trading, there are so many misconceptions, and, unfortunately, the pure lack of understanding is what either causes people to not trade in the first place or lose a lot when they do. This book is not designed or written to turn £10 into £1 billion; it's written to help you not lose money and devise a trading plan that will move you forward – regardless of the size of trading pot you start with. As the saying goes: money buys money.

All you need is a little common sense.

## TRADING AND EMOTIONS

In fact, the Trader A and Trader B I mentioned above are real people whom I know well, and their stories also illustrate how emotions are so integral to trading.

Trader A was a mentor of mine who used to work in several large investment banks, working with sums of money you'd hardly believe. Sometimes, when we would speak, he would tell me that he was a 'few million' down on his books, and you could hear the despondency in his voice. This didn't mean he wasn't a good trader; he just had to learn how to manage his emotions.

Trader B, on the other hand, only had a small account size but made consistent returns at rates most people would crave. However, she could not bear the stress of losing a single trade. As such, the account size remained at a scale that was of little value in monetary terms. Closer to home, my wife was petrified of the risk involved in trading. She would call her trades 'Starbucks bets': it would only ever make enough to buy a coffee. The thrill of the trade was there, but so was the fear. As you read later chapters, you will come to realise that emotions can be tamed and fear can be mitigated.

Greed is also a negative emotion of which you need to be aware. I had an interesting couple of sessions with a high-flying individual who had lost half a million dollars trading Ethereum and Bitcoin. He realised that he had made mistake after mistake, and he wanted to learn a route to earn the losses back. This is another major issue you tend to find in the trading space – fuelled by greed, this will eventually catch up with you and amount to losses.

When you come to understand more about the processes, the issues and dogma attached to trading, you can view what you are doing in a more objective way. I'm not saying you won't fear making a trade, or that you'll feel the urge to go from zero to 100 miles per hour as quickly as possible, but you'll get more self-awareness and, as a result, be able to manage these feelings better.

As such, I have tried to make *Master the Art of Trading* as simple as possible to follow in a chronology that will help you create your personal strategy. Some of you will struggle with fear; others will be exhilarated by a trade loss. Some of you will want to jump to level 10. However – think *Karate Kid*: 'Wax on, wax off' – you need to build a foundation first before risking a single penny of your hard-earned cash.

And remember, Fear + Greed = Poor Decisions.

## FIGHT OR FLIGHT

As humans, we are programmed with the fight or flight response. It's hard-wired into all of us. When it comes to trading, you will find that some of you will see the numbers on the screen go red and feel like you instantly want to close the trade. This is the fear taking over, and it's natural not to want to suffer too much of a loss. There are mechanisms to help with this; it's called a 'stop loss', which you will learn more about later.

Conversely, greed can quickly set in when the numbers are green and you're making money. You start to think, 'just a little bit more'. There's also a tool to help with this – it's called a TP, short for 'take profit'. Although you want to let profits run and cut losses short, you need to adhere to the trading plan and manage your emotions, and you will start to profit.

## THE REAL THING

The purpose of this chapter was to set the scene, cut through the misconceptions and manage expectations. Trading seems to be a widely misunderstood sector, and the image attached to it seems to be only what people have seen in films. I can assure you, it's not always the way and a lot of normal people trade daily. With the rise of technology and ease of access, it's a sector that more and more people enter. Post-Covid, many people have looked at trading as a way to subsidise earnings or even as a new career after spending time working from home.

The main issue in the industry is that it's also filled with snake-oil salesmen, people who don't care about others. They are hell-bent on selling the dream, and they make more money from YouTube videos and affiliate links than from trading. You don't need to fall for that. Once you have completed the book, you will have a solid foundation on how not to lose money, define a trading plan and, of course, manage your emotions when executing a trade.

## Chapter 3

# KNOW THYSELF!

Many new traders pile straight into the charts, placing trades before they know anything like enough. This is what basic trading courses encourage, and it is an astoundingly bad idea. Every trader needs to do two things first. Firstly, they need to set up a trading plan and, secondly and most importantly, they need to understand themselves because psychology plays a huge role in trading. As I've already expressed in this book, it is human nature to feel fear, greed, excitement, anger and depression. You feel all of these emotions when making a trade. It is how great traders deal with these inevitable states that makes the difference.

## PSYCHOLOGY

Let's start with the psychology element first. When analysing your own psychology, you need to understand what type of trader you are. Do you want to be in and out of the trade within seconds, minutes or a couple of hours at best? This makes you a *scalper* in trading terms. Would you prefer to watch the screen less and be out of the trade a few hours to a day or two later? This makes you a *day trader*. Perhaps it is *swing trading* that will suit you best, where you are happy to hold positions for a few days through to several weeks? Or do you see yourself as an *investor*, where your strategy is most likely to 'buy and hold' for an extended period?

Before looking at any kind of strategy or tool, being able to identify the type of trading you will be doing is key. Factors such as your job will affect what you can do, along with your psychology. Many people cannot buy and hold for long periods of time due to the stress and fear that trading like this can cause. Possibly there may be financial restraints that also affect your ability to trade. You might be looking for faster and more frequent returns on investment, so becoming an investor is not for you.

You might have a personality, energy and appetite that drives you to be more of a scalper wanting even quicker rewards.

As I have said, psychology is key. How many basic courses mention psychology in passing and don't acknowledge its importance? Humans are pre-programmed with a fight or flight attitude. Unfortunately, the colour of our P&L (Profit and Loss) may greatly affect our mindset. So if you see your P&L go in the red, you are likely to fight it, and if it goes green, you will likely run with it. Scalping can add so much more emotional stress than most people realise.

▼

Knowledge is power: know yourself and gain power over yourself.

To help you choose a time frame, here are some facts. Some are obvious; some are not. Your nature may well be such that you think you already know what type of trader you are, but make sure to look at these points and don't pretend they do not exist. They do, and they have a real impact on your bottom line.

There is a spread between the bid and the offer, the price you can sell at and the price at which you can buy. Let's say it is 1 pip, which is the unit of measurement to express the change in value between two currencies. If you are trying to capture 10 pips in a trade, which is typical for a scalper, you need to give away 10% of everything you make before you even start. The more pips you are trying to capture (which is related to the time frame you trade), the less relevant this is, and although 10% may not seem like a lot, it is very significant in a business where being right 55% of the time is seen as a big edge.

News announcements and economic figures, expected or not, will affect the shorter time frames far more than longer ones. Remember that when you are trading on short time frames, you are basically trading noise. On long time frames, the effect of news events on price looks just like that – noise – and it will balance out over time. However, if you are only trying to capture 10 or 20 pips, then that noise just blew you out of a trade, one way or another. Have you ever noticed how much more likely you are to lose than win when this happens? I have. Besides, during the rollover period (when overnight and weekend spreads alter), spreads can widen out a LOT. You can be stopped out 20 pips away from your stop. Yes. You can. It's just tough. One trader I know has a record of 55 pips away from a stop. (If this happens, contact your broker and ask nicely that they reinstate the trade.)

There is one plus to short-time-frame trading, and that is that you are not in the trade for long, so you may experience reduced pressure. Some people would rather endure many short bursts of pressure than a few long days or weeks of pressure as the price meanders about, some days going your way and other days making you sweat. You can sleep at night with no positions open. However . . .

. . . some would say the opposite. If you trade a lot, you will get a lot of losing trades, and losing trades cause psychological damage that can be hard to control. You probably know which type of mindset you have.

The other factor to consider is the 'fun' of it. It's pointless pretending that trading isn't a money game. It is. A lot of us get pleasure out of playing that game, and the more we trade, the more 'pleasure' is available. Gambling games can be very addictive. Be aware of this. I even have some advice for you if you feel you are affected: trade in very small amounts to get rid of the pressure to be in a trade all the time, and save the big bets for the good trades that come along every few days or weeks.

Swing traders can wait weeks or months for a trade. Some people don't like to wait; they want to trade. This is generally a poor attitude to have if you want to make consistent money. Patience is extremely important for all traders, but particularly for swing traders. If you do not have and cannot learn patience, then shorter-term trading will be more attractive to you.

I have not written this to make short-term traders feel foolish or to force people into longer-term trading. It's just human nature; you need to keep this in the back of your mind to break through it. I won't advocate one strategy over another as the factors come down to the individual. It's personal to you. It's your life circumstance, your job, how much time you have, your ability to deal with stress, and how much time you want to be staring at a screen each day.

Later in the book, I will describe what I do when trading, and at that stage, you will see that my personality is best suited to making relatively few low-risk swing trades rather than operating as a scalper. This makes me a natural swing trader. Many scalping strategies are successful and profitable. Many are not. But this applies to investing and swing strategies just the same.

My point is, think about the type of trader you are most likely to be because what you want and what you think you can achieve might not be what might be best suited to your personality and circumstances.

## MIND GAMES

How does psychology fit on a chart?

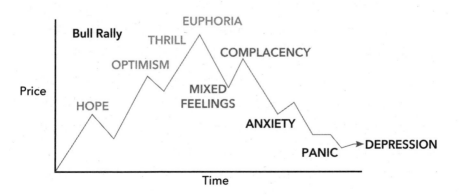

The image above is adapted from a chart known as the 'Wall Street cheat sheet', showing the emotional cycle traders go through during the market phases. If you study any of the major trading theories like Elliott Wave, Gann, Wyckoff, Dow or Fibonacci, you will find that they are all based on the psychology of human behaviour. For example, Fibonacci studied the ratios he repeatedly found in the natural world. Market prices, where there are millions of participants, are natural processes driven by human behaviour. We will cover this in more detail in a later chapter.

Although the idea is simple – buy the bottoms and sell the tops – the type of trading you do will depend on how you manage your emotions during each phase. As the market is fractal (this means that the charts look the same as you zoom in further and further), you will see this in any time frame. For this example, assume a buy (long) position. You hope the market is going up, you get excited, and optimism sets in when the trade is going in your favour. At this point, some traders cash out. This is due to fear of the market reversing against them, the fear of being wrong. However, many traders stay in and greed takes over. Thrill turns into euphoria and then *boom!* We saw this recently with Bitcoin. (In fact, I posted in March 2021 explaining the logic for a drop in the Bitcoin price: logic as to why $30,000 was a downside target. The call was made when the price was around $62,500.) You get to see the same emotional analysis play out on any chart, over and over again.

My grandfather always used to say, 'If things don't change, they will stay the same.' His advice never made sense to me as a kid but feels more than relevant today. Human emotions and psychology as a whole are not going to change any time soon. However, market conditions and instruments can be replaced. Markets are driven by human emotions and importantly, institutional traders know this. Later in this book, I will touch on this and a related concept known as Composite Man.

How often have you been in a losing trade and moved the stop loss to 'give it room to breathe', or averaged down and added to the position, or in a winning trade, bailed and seen the price move another 10, 20 or even 100 pips in your direction? That is YOUR psychology, right there laid bare. You will need to nurture the ability to have faith in your technical analysis and the proper risk management to turn losers into winners.

I've been trading for over 20 years. I can say 100% you will never beat your emotions. Humans are hard-wired; all you can do is learn to manage them the best you can. There will always be losses; it's how you deal with them emotionally that matters.

'I BELIEVE IN ANALYSIS
AND NOT FORECASTING.'
*NICOLAS DARVAS*

## Chapter 4

# THE TRADING PLAN

Now that you have identified the type of trading that suits you, the next phase of a trading plan is assessing the market.

When assessing markets, there are three main schools of thought that you need to be aware of:

1. Fundamental analysis
2. Technical analysis
3. Sentiment analysis

## FUNDAMENTAL ANALYSIS

Fundamental analysis is essentially a study of company records, financial reports and other areas, such as sector fundamentals and news flow. You can assess a company without seeing a chart. How many more sales did the company make this year compared to last? What is the forecast for next year's sales?

You could even make an investment decision based on an event. For example, during global lockdowns due to the Covid-19 outbreak, flights were grounded. Air travel is the biggest user of oil, so oil demand went down, and the price of the commodity dropped. This is just one example of how using the news can be a benefit for trading fundamentals. I could extend this into the crypto-currency market. If, for example, there is news that Tesla wants to use Bitcoin as a form of payment, although it is not a driver, it will help the hype as many retail traders will buy on the back of the positive news. The inverse is also true. A tweet by the CEO saying now Tesla won't use Bitcoin may mean panic sets in, and many naïve traders will sell out.

**'If most traders would learn to sit on their hands 50 percent of the time, they would make a lot more money.'**

**Bill Lipschutz**

## TECHNICAL ANALYSIS

Technical analysis (TA) is a technical study of the charts. This includes any way you can analyse a price, like looking just at price action (a wide-ranging term meaning ignoring other indicators), using averages and other indicators. You do it all in an attempt to make a more informed trading decision. Many technical analysis techniques claim superiority, but again, this will come down to the individual and their psychology.

There is so much subjectivity to technical analysis that you could buy, and I could sell, and we could both be correct because my strategy is long term, and you are reading the charts as a scalper. What many online courses won't teach you is the broader view. They have their methods, and it's all so black and white. All technical analyses should come with a disclaimer and emphasise that emotions play a huge role in whether or not the strategy will be successful for each individual.

Again, there is potential to go down a huge rabbit hole on this topic, which I won't be doing here. Just bias whatever TA you do towards the style that suits your temperament as technical analysis also includes emotional analysis. This concerns theories of human behaviour, which will form a large part of your decision-making.

## SENTIMENT ANALYSIS

The last largely recognised type of analysis is sentiment. Analysing the sentiment means obtaining the opinion of the masses or using tools such as weekly Commitments of Traders (COT) reports. As a sentiment trader, you would often want to be contrarian to the sentiment of the retail traders. After all, over 75% of retail traders lose money. So, doing the opposite seems to me to be a better idea.

Now we have covered the main three schools of thought regarding assessing the markets, we need to consider two further things that you'll need to embed these into your trading plan. The first is risk management, and the second is what's called the 1% Rule.

## RISK MANAGEMENT

The next part of creating a trading plan is risk management, and this deserves your full attention. When you think of risk management, remember that it's not only designed to keep you in the game, it's also a useful tool for better profits when used correctly.

> **'I have two basic rules about winning in trading as well as in life:**
> 1. **If you don't bet, you can't win.**
> 2. **If you lose all your chips, you can't bet.'**
>
> **Larry Hite**

Let's talk about the reward to risk ratio (RR).

If you set your stop loss (SL) and take profit (TP) so that you could win or lose $100, this is an RR of 1:1.

If you have this as part of your base strategy, you would need to be more than 50% accurate to make money. (I am also ignoring spread costs and other incidentals like commission and swap costs, but that is fine for now.)

Assume that $100 is 1% of a $10,000 account. In theory, if you risk 1% of an account and lose the first trade, your next trade will only be 1% of the new balance, gradually decreasing the risk asymptotically. And then the opposite applies when winning, leading to exponential growth. If you make just under 2% per month nice and steady, your pot should double in three years. And double again three years later. And . . . this is obvious by now, right?

Let's simplify this concept further.

If I have a 50% win rate and I'm willing to lose $100 every time if it goes wrong but make $100 on every win, I would be regarded as a break-even trader.

To increase the odds in my favour, I can do one of two things:

1. Become more accurate (win more than 50%)
2. Increase the reward ratio to my risk

Let's assume I do number 1. All I need is a 51% win rate, and I could expect to make money overall. Increasing to a 60% win rate gives me decent profits. The more the percentage of winning trades increases, the more I make. Remember, this is with an RR of 1.

How about trying method number 2?

If I am willing to lose $100 but now only take trades with an expected 2:1 ratio, this means that, if I am willing to lose $100 on my losers, I expect to take $200 from my winners.

This means that, even at a strike rate of 50%, I am very profitable. If you assume I lose five trades at $100 each time and make $200 on my five winners, I have a net gain of $500. Alternatively, you could think of every win 'paying for two losses'.

What if I could get a better win rate than 50% AND have a better reward ratio than 1:1?

This is why a trading plan is important.

Having a 3:1 reward to risk ratio means that you can technically be wrong 70% of the time and still be profitable. The more this is refined, the better the profits. This sets you off on the route to becoming a professional trader.

Planning your trade is a vital prerequisite to successful trading.

Setting the stop loss ensures you know what you are prepared to lose before entering the trade.

Effectively, risk management is capital preservation. It is a crucial part of your trading plan as it helps to ensure you manage your funds properly.

> **'Confidence is not "I will profit on this trade."**
> **Confidence is "I will be fine if I don't profit from**
> **this trade."'**
>
> **Yvan Byeajee**

## THE 1% RULE AND THE '90-90-90 RULE'

I suggest when you start trading, only risk 1% per trade. In fact, even established traders should only risk 1%. I am deliberately recommending this. Why?

Did you know that there is an unwritten rule in the trading world known as the '90-90-90 rule'?

This means that statistically, 90% of new traders lose 90% of their accounts within 90 days of starting out.

Think about this for a second. It doesn't sound very positive, does it?

However, if you use proper risk management, you could lose seven trades in a row, win the next three and still profit.

Even established traders get complacent or cocky and often double down on losing trades, and soon the risk is 5% or 10% or more.

How much is it possible to make when only risking 1% at a time? Keep your profits in the account so that you can use the exponential growth in your favour.

Why not use the 1% to create a pot that, in essence, funds your trading so that it pays for itself? This could help eliminate emotional attachment to the monetary value that you have invested and future losses.

**'Amateurs think about how much money they can make. Professionals think about how much money they could lose.'**

**Jack Schwager**

Before moving on to the next phase, you should define your trading style:

☐ Scalper

☐ Day Trader

☐ Swing Trader

☐ Investor

You can always change later, but if you don't set a goal or have a clearly defined path, then you are less likely to succeed.

'I'M NOT LOST, I'VE JUST
TEMPORARILY LOST SIGHT
OF MY DESTINATION.'

*UNKNOWN*

## Chapter 5

# STRATEGY CREATION

Now you have a trading plan. You have identified the type of trader you are from the style and timeframe to the type of analysis that would suit your personality best.

Risk management needs to be a consideration, and you need to think of it logically and reasonably.

Next is identifying the instrument that you will trade. Are you interested in trading cryptocurrency, forex, indices, commodities or stocks? Or are you interested in trading a mixture? It doesn't really matter as these techniques work on any instrument to a degree.

Note that crypto has not been around very long, so there is limited data. Less data means that price action may be less representative of how the instrument will behave in the future.

This book was written to give you an edge and the confidence to assess the market, follow a systematic approach and profit from your trading.

## CREATING A PROFITABLE STRATEGY

Creating a profitable strategy is hard. I'll show you how I trade in order to inform your own strategy but, more importantly, I will show you how *I think*. Your strategy might be different from mine because you are different from me. With any book you read on trading, I recommend you take away the parts that work for you.

These are all the parts that worked for me.

I recommend that you read to the end of the book before making any trades based on anything you learn here.


## STRATEGY CREATION

What affects the price of whatever you are trading?

Personally, I like to break things down. Sometimes I even put them back together. The idea is to understand various elements, covering the fundamental and technical analysis, giving you an edge.

If you are looking to trade an altcoin, it will make sense to watch Bitcoin. You can gain information on Bitcoin by scanning the news, for example, or by using Bitcoin as an indicator on your altcoin chart. It could be by obtaining sentiment from other communities or larger altcoins such as XRP and Ethereum to get a feel for what the market is saying. (See Chapter 7 for a technique to use when assessing an alt coin.)

Assessing a forex pair or a commodity would be the same. Looking at pairs that include USD (including most commodities priced in dollars), it makes sense to take the time to assess what the DXY (the US Dollar Index) is doing. You can deploy the same techniques on the DXY to potentially spot signs or patterns that will affect other instruments. Instead of Bitcoin (BTC) being the key to the overall market sentiment, you need to know if the US government is hawkish or dovish on the dollar – again, sentiment and technical working hand in hand. A lot of this is simply logic, and you will learn this with experience. When some assets go up, naturally others will fall. This of course is due to the whole economy being traded against something else – gold for cash, coffee for dollars, a Bitcoin for some altcoin.

If you are looking at a stock, you most likely want to have a broad idea of the company's financials – even if you're more of a technical analyst. It's not going to hurt. You should be able to understand a profit and loss statement and a balance sheet at a minimum, so you know the risks the company faces and its general economic health.

This is the basis for any instrument that you decide to trade. At first, stick to around three to five currency pairs, or stocks, or whatever instrument you are working with, and get to know them over months. This will help you understand the character: I often tell people that it's like learning a foreign language. You might find it difficult to learn all of Russian, Japanese and German at the same time.

Monitor them, back-test them and become familiar with them. This is why less is more!

You may not realise this, but they all have different character-istics, and they move differently in volatile markets.

For fundamentals and news, all you need to know is that

news is already built into price – most of the larger operators and institutional investors know the news before it becomes news. So apart from global catastrophic events, the price and price direction already reflect the news flow and sentiment of the market overall. News just serves to confuse.

Even when you have an event such as mass lockdowns due to Covid-19, for some instruments you can see that the price hit a level it was already expected to hit. It just arrived a little earlier.

'ALL NEW NEWS IS OLD
NEWS, HAPPENING TO
NEW PEOPLE.'
         *MALCOLM MUGGERIDGE*

# Chapter 6

# TECHNICAL ANALYSIS

As I mentioned in the introduction, the idea of this book is to give traders a starting point. If you are completely new to trading, you can now identify the type of trader you are, you know the type of analysis best suited to your goals, and have a grasp of sentiment and the fundamentals.

Technical analysis is a whole new ball game! People have their own preferred methods, indicators and time frames.

So, it's not about identifying one method as better than another – all you need is a little common sense, mixed with some simple logic.

Let's start with the basics.

## TREND LINES

Below are examples of trend lines, which show the prevailing movement of a price, and which many readers may already be familiar with. The quickest way to identify a trend is to zoom out and look at the direction.

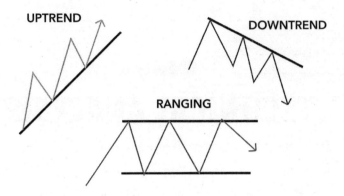

In an uptrend, you must simply connect the lows. In a downtrend, connect the highs. When ranging – where the price is moving back and forth – draw a horizontal line connecting the tops and another connecting the bottoms.

Charts never move in straight lines. You will quickly notice that higher highs and higher lows equal an uptrend, and lower highs and lower lows create a downtrend, as you can see from the diagram below.

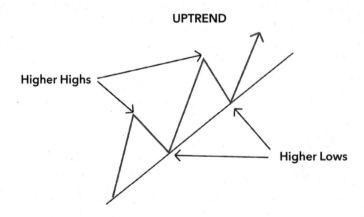

Although the concept of trend lines is a simple one, there are many arguments in the industry as to how you draw them properly. The truth is, it does not matter. What you are looking for is direction rather than a subjective line between points. Can it help? Well, yes. Do they make money? Well, not really, not on their own.

Over the years, I have studied all kinds of tools, bots and indicators, and what I have come to appreciate is that less is often more. Know enough to get what you need. You can research trend lines and go into all kinds of really awesome techniques such as Tom DeMark's count and proportion beyond the trend. I am not saying these methods don't work. They often do, and it can be very useful to know them in depth as you progress in your proficiency as a trader. But do you need it? I would say no.

I have a lot of respect for in-depth methods, and it's worth studying them if you like to know all the ins and outs of things. However, for the purpose of keeping this book as useful as possible to the novice trader, I'm going to mention these things and skip a lot of the unnecessary details.

Trend lines are all about identifying bias – is it going up or down? When used with other techniques, they can give you more insight.

'BULL MARKETS ARE BORN
ON PESSIMISM, GROW ON
SKEPTICISM, MATURE
ON OPTIMISM AND DIE ON
EUPHORIA.'
                SIR JOHN TEMPLETON

# Chapter 7

# FUNDAMENTAL ANALYSIS

## AN ALTCOIN

As an example of fundamental analysis, let's talk about how to assess an altcoin. I've decided to choose this type of analysis rather than using technical analysis because of the fact that there might be enough usable information in the charts. So understanding the team, the goal, the funding rounds – essentially all of the fundamentals – will help assess the value of the project.

The amount of technical analysis possible with such limited data available on the charts is relatively small.

Below we can see a chart showing the moving average.

This image has a faint line, which is actually the moving average of the price. If you look closely, there is a moving average on this chart. It's about as much use as an ice cube in the desert. There is simply not enough data to make it significant.

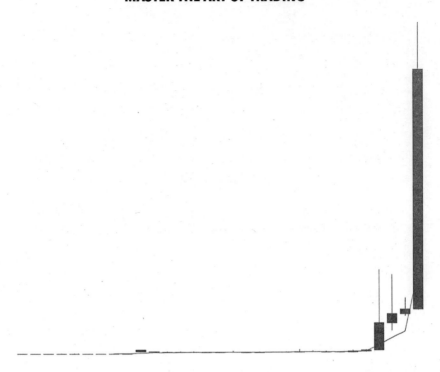

Some technical analysis methods have been inherited from the legacy financial markets. Many new crypto traders use the same technical indicators seen in forex, stocks and commodities trading.

You often see tools such as RSI (relative strength index), MACD (moving average convergence/divergence) and Bollinger Bands. They all seek to predict market behaviour. The issue with all these, when applied to crypto, is the lack of price data, as mentioned above. Yet, these technical analysis tools are extremely popular in the cryptocurrency space, which goes against all logic. It's slightly harder to give a moving average much credence when the price is in a 90-degree move up, and the RSI of a 12-month-old coin means almost nothing.

Therefore, fundamental analysis works best as a starting point for cryptocurrency, though the approach is similar to that used in legacy markets.

When analysing a coin, you need to appreciate that it is still a company, after all, so your fundamental analysis should include taking a deep dive into the available information, as it would for any other company you are considering trading on. You would want to review the project use case, the team and the money the project has raised so far.

Your goal is to reach a conclusion on whether the asset is overvalued or undervalued. At that stage, you can use your insights to inform your trading positions. For example, have you had a major hype period, so that a dump can now be expected? Or you might ask yourself the question: why would the market makers, banks and exchange want you to buy at the top? If trading was that easy, wouldn't you think everyone would be a trader?

You can't really use tried-and-tested forex tools to assess crypto assets. To conduct a proper analysis, what you need is to understand where they derive value from.

Cryptocurrency networks can't be assessed through the same lens as traditional businesses. If anything, the more decentralised offerings like Bitcoin are closer to commodities in some sense. But even with the more centralised cryptocurrencies, such as those issued by organisations, traditional fundamental analysis indicators can't tell us much.

So, now you are stuck between a rock and a hard place.

A quick early step would be to identify strong metrics. These should not take into account things like Twitter or Facebook followers because it's so easy these days to buy several thousand followers for social media sites. You should keep this in mind with everything news-related.

One method could be to count the number of active addresses on a blockchain and see if it has been sharply increasing. You wouldn't be able to get information like this about a stock, but you can with crypto, so why not use what you can get? Use whatever information is available.

Are you seeing company principals transferring money back and forth to themselves with new addresses each time? This is the level of info you can go down to – this is the blockchain, after all.

If you want to get a bit more technical, you can look at 'on-chain' metrics in depth. On-chain metrics are those that can be observed by looking at data provided by the blockchain itself.

Running a node for the desired crypto and examining the data can be time-consuming and expensive, particularly if you are only considering the investment and don't want to waste time or resources on this process.

In some instances, a simple way to do this is to use API-based solutions, plug into exchanges and use third-party tools, such as Binance Research project reports.

Look for information such as:

1. Active addresses
2. Transaction value
3. Fees

If this all sounds like a lot of work – well, it is – but did you really expect to get away with it without taking it seriously? It's the same as spending a year learning to trade instead of just three weeks. You have to spend time and effort to progress.

If you are thinking of buying the coin, you are basically 'investing' in a tech company, which is the long and short of it. So, go and read through the white paper until you understand it. After all, if you don't understand something, then why would you invest in it? You shouldn't get wrapped up in the hype. It will eventually come back to kick you. Assess use cases and business models. Do they make sense to you? Do the company and market make commercial sense? You are likely to be just as good at seeing common sense as any guru analyst. Trust your thoughts. You don't want to be saying in six months, 'I thought that was a dumb idea.'

Next, go even deeper and review the team. Do they have experience? Have they already raised enough capital to keep the project going long enough to succeed? In a lot of countries, all companies are listed on a register. In the UK, for example, you can look up any company on the Companies House web portal, so you can see details of shareholders and directors, and look into their past business efforts to see if they have succeeded.

You should also consider the level of competition in the space. What projects are offering similar solutions, and are the other companies further along? Does the company you are looking at have some kind of advantage over their competitors? Maybe a unique selling point (USP)?

Finally, consider initial distribution and tokenomics as a whole. A lot of projects have created tokens as a solution looking for a problem. Dogecoin, on the other hand, created a meme for the market, which is turning into a solution.

Understanding the use case cannot be stressed enough. As such, it's important to determine whether the token has real utility. Will it have decent adoption? The backing of major players or corporations is a good sign.

Consider how the funds were initially distributed. Was it via an ICO or IEO, or could users earn it by mining?

The white paper should outline how much is kept for the founders and team and how much will be available to investors. If it was mined, you could look for evidence of the asset creator doing some pre-mining (mining on the network before it's announced).

Much like assessments of companies, altcoins will have information that you can extract. However, remember that only you can make the decision as to their value. A good team, a good product will not always mean the company or the coin will be successful.

'YOU GET RECESSIONS, YOU HAVE STOCK MARKET DECLINES. IF YOU DON'T UNDERSTAND THAT'S GOING TO HAPPEN, THEN YOU'RE NOT READY, YOU WON'T DO WELL IN THE MARKETS.'

*PETER LYNCH*

## Chapter 8

# INDICATORS

Many new traders start with indicators: statistics that measure current condition and then also look ahead to forecast financial or economic trends. Whilst useful, they can also be distracting. Most indicators lag, which means you're only getting info already written on the chart. Just keep this in mind, especially when someone tries to pitch you a fully automated system with a 90% win rate. If it were that easy, the world would be lacking police officers, firefighters, doctors and nurses, and postal workers. They would all be sipping sangria on a beach somewhere as professional algo-traders.

Here are some of the basics, should you want to include them in your technical analysis.

## MOVING AVERAGES

Some readers will have used moving averages or at least know them. This is an indicator that is used to determine the trend direction. Again, much like trend lines, there is room for them some of the time. Do you really need them? No.

I have been having this discussion more and more since coming back to education a second time. Again, let's exemplify this using Bitcoin.

At the time of writing, Bitcoin has had more than a four-year bull run. What do you think a moving average is going to tell you?

Will it tell you that yesterday's price was lower than today's? Of course not! It will simply tell you that it is above the moving average.

Some people will use a moving average as a sign of either support or resistance, but this then takes us back to the psychological aspect – it's a self-fulfilling prophecy. Humans are designed to identify patterns and cycles even when they do not exist.

Whether it's shapes in the sky made by the stars at night or the alleged 'support level' of a few major moving averages, the issue with these is that if you simply change the setting; it becomes a different level.

Look for places where the price action ignored the moving average. What happened there then? Isn't it more likely that the price reacted to something that just happened to be on or near a moving average?

This is the perfect example of seeing a pattern that may not even be there. I can show you countless examples of where a price seems to be respectful of a 50- or 200-period moving average, but it has nothing to do with it at all. It just looks like it does.

Many so-called gurus are actually not traders, but they will plug techniques like moving average crosses.

You might have heard of the term 'death cross'. Some self-confessed experts will use a 50-moving average crossing below a 200, for example, to indicate a selling signal. A sudden correction in a long uptrend will give this signal after the correction has already happened! They are betting that the correction is a long one or even the start of a reversal. I'd bet they are able to make a RR (risk-to-reward) of 1:1 on it about 50% of the time.

All of this support and resistance logic is actually available when studying pure price action, without the use of any indicators at all. You could do a lot worse than to switch all your moving averages off right now and just look at price action without being distracted by them. All you are really aiming to find is a general bias.

## OTHER TYPES OF INDICATORS

Other off-the-shelf indicators such as Bollinger Bands, relative strength index (RSI) are used by the vast majority of retail traders – the same group losing over 75% of the time.

Mark Cuban once said, 'Everyone is a genius in a bull market.'

This kind of sums it up nicely. An RSI, for example, is a trending yet lagging indicator. So, you are getting confirmation of a trend. Yet, trends are generally obvious from price. Also, remember this is another lagging indicator, so you are seeing yesterday's information today.

All I am trying to emphasise is to not depend on them.

Indicators should be used more to assist and not to identify. This means that they add to or subtract from the evidence.

People are often too lazy to learn. People want a buy-me-now, sell-me-now type of indicator. Sadly, if there was an accurate one, wouldn't the owner just keep it to themselves?

Don't take this as purely negative or anti-algorithms and indicators – it's just pointing out the obvious.

**'Look left.'**

**Lewis Daniels (also possibly many other educators and professional traders)**

## INDICATORS – THE LOGIC

I often laugh when someone says, 'If it is above the 200-day EMA (the 200-day exponential moving average), it's an uptrend.'

Imagine being long in the position from point A to point B:

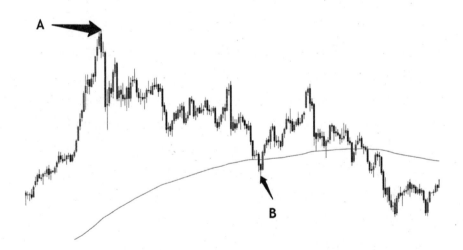

In this chart above you can see that, although the price action is above the moving average, it's falling.

Looking at price action, you would clearly see a downtrend

from point A to point B and wait for a clear change of character for a long entry. The 200 EMA is therefore not relevant here.

## RSI VS. STOCHASTIC

Another interesting argument I see, over and over, is the use of an indicator at the wrong time. It is important to know what an indicator does rather than just applying it to a chart. Too often, gurus teach that one strategy fits all market conditions. This could not be further from the truth.

As an example, let's look at the argument for stochastics over RSI. Keeping things simple, a stochastic is based on momentum, and is useful for choppy and sideways markets, whereas an RSI is useful for a trending move. In theory, using an RSI in a counter-trend move is as much use as a chocolate teapot.

Whilst there are strategies and techniques you can apply, the stochastic would be a better indicator to use given the market conditions. When the market flips, and you can clearly see impulsive, trending moves, the RSI is very useful for spotting trend continuation trades – like spotting the end of a pullback – or indicating the end of a trend as an exit strategy.

To summarise, the relative strength index (RSI) was designed to measure the relative speed of trending price movements.

The stochastic is more like a measure of the pendulum's swing in a choppy or ranging market.

Another off-the-shelf indicator new traders like to use is the MACD, which stands for moving average convergence/ divergence.

This is simply a trend-following oscillator. It predominantly shows the relationship between the price and the moving averages. Its standard settings are 26 and 12, which is the 26 EMA (exponential moving average) subtracted from the 12 EMA, which creates the 'trigger' line.

You then have a 9 EMA, and that line is then called the 'signal' line. And in essence, when one crosses the other, a trader would use it as a buy or sell signal.

MACD is usually displayed with a histogram that graphs the distance between the MACD and its signal line.

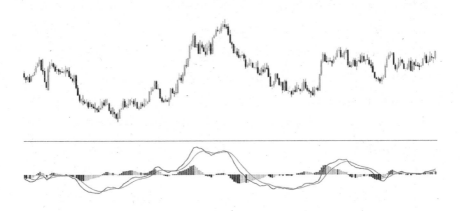

In this image above, you will see the light grey histogram when the market is trending upwards and the dark grey histogram when the market moves to the downside. The purpose of this book is not to teach the MACD. I am trying to acknowledge the fact that many traders would have seen this indicator or, at some time or another, been introduced to it.

Like most indicators, it's another lagging, not a leading

indicator, which means you can obtain a lot of the information from the chart and the simple price action.

Indicators are not always obvious and not always on the charts. One such tool I like to use is the Commitments of Traders report.

## COMMITMENTS OF TRADERS REPORT (COT)

The Commitments of Traders (COT) report is a weekly publication that shows the aggregate holdings of different participants in the US futures market. Published every Friday by the Commodity Futures Trading Commission (CFTC), the COT report is a snapshot of the commitment of the classified trading groups as of Tuesday that same week.

The report provides investors with almost up-to-date information on futures market operations and increases the transparency of these complex exchanges. Many futures traders use it as a market signal on which to base trading decisions.

The COT report shows how many long, short and spread positions make up the open interest. There are four different COT reports, comprising legacy, supplemental, disaggregated and traders in financial futures.

I have developed my own COT report, which is now also running as an algorithm. The figures are uploaded in chart form on Fridays for us to analyse over the weekend.

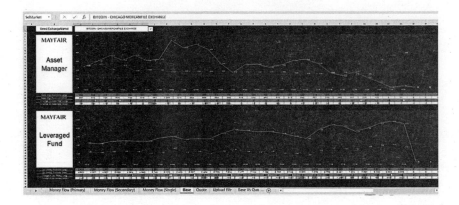

Above is the Mayfair COT report, showing a chart form of the current reportable institutional long and short positions.

The standard reports are read as tables, with each row and column labelled appropriately. Note that the latest information is on the **left-hand side** of the report.

The information in the report indicates how much interest there is, both long and short, in various derivatives contracts and which type of market actor is involved. The main actors are:

1. Commercial
2. Non-commercial

And then, from there, you can break the report down further. This would include:

## A Producer/Merchant/Processor/User

An entity that predominantly engages in the production, processing, packing or handling of a physical commodity and uses the futures markets to manage or hedge risks associated with those activities.

## A Swap Dealer

An entity that deals primarily in swaps for a commodity and uses the futures markets to manage or hedge the risk associated with those swaps' transactions. The swap dealer's counterparties may be speculative traders, like hedge funds, or traditional commercial clients that are managing risk arising from their dealings in the physical commodity.

## A Money Manager

For the purpose of this report this is a registered commodity trading advisor (CTA), a registered commodity pool operator (CPO) or an unregistered fund identified by the CFTC. These traders are engaged in managing and conducting organised futures trading on behalf of clients.

## Other Reportable

This comprises every other reportable trader that is not placed into one of the other three categories is placed into the 'other reportable' category.

## WHY IS THIS USEFUL?

In summary, we know that retail tends to lose money and that large operators often make huge profits. COT data can assist you in understanding where the higher percentage of winners are likely to be trading. It's a window into what the big boys are doing. It's not super-accurate and only covers futures markets, so it has limited breadth. However, it *is* broadly representative and is more or less our only view of institutional bias, so it is very useful.

Given this knowledge, you now have a bias for our positions. You have access to indicators such as the DXY, and you can also assess the positions, or at least the bias, of the consistent winners in the market. You have a pretty compelling story before you place any orders.

## OVERUSE

Newer students of the markets often over-use indicators. This leads to indecision and confusion, even conflict when doing technical analysis. Many new traders are looking for the 'golden' indicator – no loss, no drawdown and perfect entries and exits on every time frame. I often find traders cluttering their charts with all of the basic indicators. You then see them missing trades, as one indicator said one thing and another said something else. They missed an opportunity as a result of too much information. So, knowing what you want from each indicator you apply to your chart is crucial.

Moving away from indicators is the ideal scenario.

While they can help highlight confluence or give that extra piece of confirmation, you have to bear in mind that most losing retail traders are using these exact indicators.

Price action is king, and no indicator is going to take the crown. If you want to apply indicators to the charts, just think: less is more. And remember, knowing the purpose of each indicator is equally important. When to use an RSI or a stochastic was the perfect example of this.

# INDICATORS

As you can probably tell, I am not a huge fan of too many indicators. At Mayfair, we include them as part of our offering. Not because we believe in them, but as a method of training a student's eyes to spot what the price action is clearly already painting.

# Chapter 9

# OVERTRADING

## THE NUMBER OF TRADES

The common misconception is that more trading equals more money. Overtrading, where you have too many trades on at the same time, can hurt the mindset. Worse, it leads to trading on minimum evidence, rather than waiting for more positive signals – which can hurt the account balance.

Trading is a fool's game, so it is better to have fewer higher probability trades that are more profitable with less risk.

New traders are looking for possibilities, whilst professional traders look for probabilities. To put this simply, if you place 100 trades, you would not only have to spend a lot more screen time making your analysis effectively, but you are also adding to the emotional stress that each trade carries.

Just wait until you start to trade on shorter time frames for more entries. This flows into more instruments, and before you know it, you are the jack of all instruments and the master of none. You will end up being more reliant on instruments to make your analysis and decision-making, and lose the 'feel' of each trade.

Probabilities vs. possibilities . . .

The more info you try to analyse, the more likely you are to confuse yourself. If you're trying to keep tabs on multiple instruments, indicators and time frames, you are simply overwhelming your ability to compute the information.

Imagine trading 15 pairs on a 15-minute time frame, using 15 indicators. You will be overloaded and burnt out. Does this sound familiar? This is one of the reasons why 75% or more of retail traders repeatedly lose money.

If things don't change, they will stay the same.

As a professional trader, you want to limit your risk exposure, increase probabilities and remove some of the stress associated with placing a trade and make fewer, more high-probability lower-risk trades.

Therefore, it is best to cut down the number of instruments you want to master and deploy slightly longer time periods, allowing you more freedom and time away from the desk to decompress. This also helps you keep your mind clear when you are at the desk.

## SUMMING IT ALL UP

You now know that it is important to have a plan, and you are hopefully aware that less is often more. Fewer trades, fewer indicators and fewer instruments will help you beyond belief.

# OVERTRADING

At this point in the book, you should also have an idea of risk management.

You are also now very much aware that the best technical analysis is based on emotional analysis of human psychology – everything from where stops are placed to why new traders love indicators (and why that helps them consistently lose money).

With some of the very simple logic I have presented here, you can start to imagine how a trade will begin to look.

Hopefully, you have already started to see the charts in a very different way. Your eye should be drawn to price action and away from the moving average.

## MAYFAIR'S ADVANCED INDICATORS

As I said in the last chapter, I am not opposed to indicators and helpful tools. Here at Mayfair, we use several proprietary tools and indicators. We also sell indicators that clue you in that there may be some price movement due or that help confirm your inclination to trade a particular set-up, and that is how all indicators should be used.

We have advised from the beginning that students use them to get a feel for them and assist with spotting the obvious. Within a short time, our students get a feel for price prospects but use the indicators less and in fewer numbers.

We have indicators that are a little more technical to assist with finding Wyckoff schematics. Again, I use it as a visual aid rather than a signal generator.

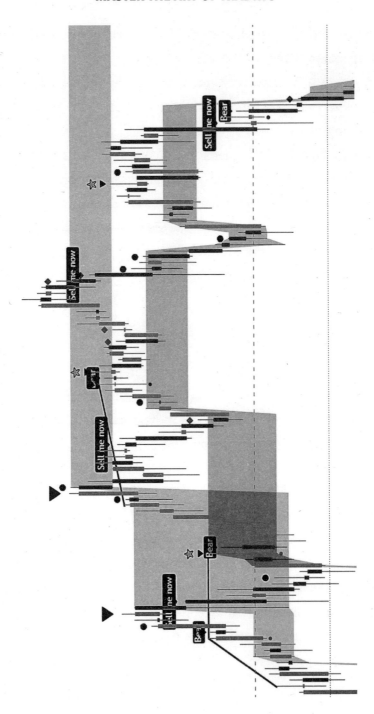

# OVERTRADING

Opposite is the 'Mayfair Wyckoff Sell' indicator in action, showing sell entries automated by software.

Even with the years of experience that have gone into creating such indicators, there will still be an emotional aspect to the analysis.

I hope you see the logic in my approach, and I hope that I am giving you the insights you need. If there's one thing I can't stress enough, it's this: Dumb it down, simplify where possible!

'THE MIND IS A FASCINATING INSTRUMENT THAT CAN MAKE OR BREAK YOU.'

YVAN BYEAJEE

# Chapter 10

# EMOTIONAL ANALYSIS

Most people will refer to Charles H. Dow, Ralph Nelson Elliott, Richard Wyckoff and William Delbert Gann as the great masters of technical analysis.

Dow was a journalist who co-founded *The Wall Street Journal*, as well as Dow Jones & Company, and, some argue, started the development of technical analysis. Elliott was an accountant who studied stock market data. Richard Wyckoff was an investor who founded the *Magazine of Wall Street*. Gann was a trader and prolific author, who developed a number of technical analysis efforts.

However, to call them masters of just technical analysis, I feel, barely scratches the surface of what they really tapped into.

Remember the 90-90-90 rule? This is compounded by people doing the same thing over and over again and expecting different results. It is essentially typical human behaviour. These great masters knew not only what was happening on the charts but also the reasons why it did. Namely: the emotional analysis of trading.

Many retail traders are using the same tools: RSI, moving averages and the like. Nothing is changing, and therefore, everything will remain the same. The same great masters of technical analysis each had their own ways of explaining elements of this.

What is also interesting is that these techniques have been around for around 100 years. When you see the logic, you will realise why I refer to Charles Dow, Ralph Elliott, Richard Wyckoff and William Delbert Gann, first and foremost, as emotional analysts studying human behaviour.

## DOW THEORY

The Dow Theory is a comprehensive 'grand theory' of technical analysis and human behaviour.

Most trading strategies used today hinge on Dow's one key concept, the 'trend', as we have already seen in our basic analysis of trends earlier on.

The trend was a novel idea when Charles Dow published his writings at the end of the 19th century. The Dow Theory says that the market is in an upward trend if one of its averages goes above a previous important high and is accompanied or followed by a similar movement in the other average. Therefore, a Dow Theory trading strategy is based on a trend-following strategy and can either be bullish or bearish.

Although the times have changed, and Dow was largely studying stock prices (particularly through his co-invention, the

Dow Jones Industrial Average), human nature and the basic principles have stayed the same, and a lot of his theory can easily be applied to instruments such as commodities, forex and crypto.

The Dow Theory is based on the analysis of maximum and minimum market fluctuations to make accurate predictions on the market's direction.

According to the Dow Theory, the importance of these upward and downward movements is their position in relation to previous fluctuations. This method teaches investors to read a trading chart and to better understand what is happening with any asset at any given moment. With this simple analysis, even the most inexperienced can identify the context in which a financial instrument is evolving.

Furthermore, Charles Dow supported the belief that an asset price and its resulting movements on a trading chart already have the necessary information available and forecasted to make accurate predictions.

Based on his theory, he co-created the Dow Jones Industrial Index and the Dow Jones Rail Index (now known as the Transportation Index), originally developed for *The Wall Street Journal*. Charles Dow created these stock indices as he believed that they would provide an accurate reflection of companies' economic and financial conditions in two major economic sectors: the industrial and the railway (transportation) sectors.

Dow Theory has six tenets:

1. The market has three movements.
   a) The 'main movement', primary movement or major trend, may last from less than a year to several years.

It can be bullish or bearish.

b) The 'medium swing', secondary reaction or intermediate reaction, may last from ten days to three months and generally retraces from 33% to 66% of the primary price change since the previous medium swing or the start of the main movement.

c) The 'short swing' or minor movement varies with opinion from hours to a month or more. The three movements may be simultaneous – for instance, a daily minor movement in a bearish secondary reaction in a bullish primary movement.

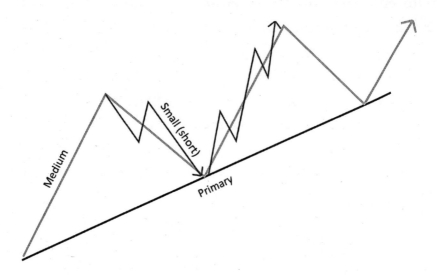

Here we can see the three major trends: the primary trend in black, the medium-term trend in light grey, and the shorter-term trend in dark grey. You can see they are fractal in nature and you have trends within trends.

2. Market trends have three phases. The Dow Theory asserts that major market trends consist of three phases: an accumulation phase, a public participation phase and a distribution phase. Let's use a bull market as an example.

  a) The accumulation phase (phase 1) is a period when investors 'in the know' are actively buying stock against the general opinion of the market. During this phase, the stock price does not change much because these investors are in the minority demanding (absorbing) stock that the market at large is supplying (releasing).

  b) Eventually, the market catches on to these astute investors and a rapid price change follows (phase 2). This occurs when trend followers and other technically oriented investors participate and ends with rampant speculation.

  c) At this point, the astute investors begin to distribute their holdings to the market (phase 3).

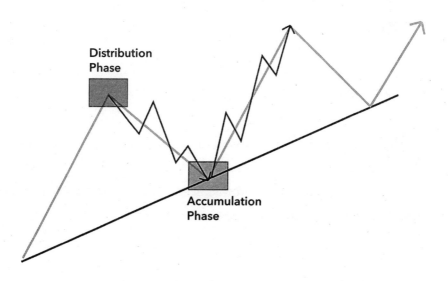

This image above shows where you can expect distribution and accumulation phases to occur – think of them like a warehouse: when the price is cheap (wholesale) you would expect the warehouse to accumulate, and to sell at (retail) higher prices.

Note the phases above. This will now repeat from accumulation to the next distribution, which is the mark up or down, also known as the 'public participation phase'.

3. The stock market discounts all news. Stock prices quickly incorporate new information as soon as it becomes available. Once news is released, stock prices will change to reflect this new information. On this point, the Dow Theory states the news is already built into the price.

4. Stock market averages must confirm one another. In Dow's time, the US was a growing industrial power. The US had population centres, but factories were scattered throughout the country. Factories had to ship their goods to market, usually by rail. Dow's first stock averages were an index of industrial (manufacturing) companies and rail companies. To Dow, a bull market in industrials could not occur unless the railway average rallied as well, usually first. According to this logic, if manufacturers' profits are rising, it follows that they are producing more.

   If they produce more, then they have to ship more goods to consumers. Hence, if an investor is looking for signs of health in manufacturers, he or she should look at the performance of the companies that ship their output to market – the railroads. The two averages should be moving in the same direction. When the performance of the two averages diverges, it is a warning that change is in the air.

Both *Barron's* magazine and *The Wall Street Journal* still publish the daily performance of the Dow Jones Transportation Average in chart form. The index contains major railroads, shipping companies and air freight carriers in the US.

5. Trends are confirmed by volume. Dow believed that volume confirmed price trends. When prices move on low volume, there could be many different explanations. An overly aggressive seller could be present, for example. But when price movements are accompanied by high volume, Dow believed this represented the 'true' market view.

    If many participants are active in a particular security, and the price moves significantly in one direction, Dow maintained that this was the direction in which the market anticipated continued movement. To him, it was a signal that a trend was developing.

6. Trends exist until definitive signals prove that they have ended. Dow believed that trends existed despite 'market noise'. Markets might temporarily move opposite the trend, but they will soon resume the prior move. The trend should be given the benefit of the doubt during these reversals.

    Determining whether a reversal is the start of a new trend or a temporary movement in the current trend is not easy. Dow theorists often disagree in this determination. Technical analysis tools attempt to clarify this, but they can be interpreted differently by different investors.

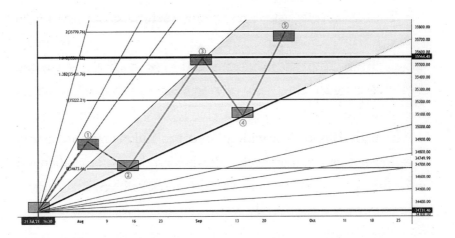

The chart above shows the Dow Theory and the Great Masters techniques combined. It might look complex here, but I can assure you that over the next couple of chapters, you will know how to apply these techniques for yourself.

In simple form, the Dow Theory is a 'wrap' or a 'frame' for most known technical analyses.

**'The main purpose of the stock market is to make fools of as many men as possible.'**

**Bernard Baruch**

## ELLIOTT WAVE THEORY

While the Dow Theory is great for looking at the whole picture, the Elliott Wave Theory can be used to look at the cycles. R.N. Elliott also knew the importance of Fibonacci levels, how humans will interact with these levels, which then go on to form waves or cycles.

Elliott posited that crowd psychology essentially creates 'mood swings', which then create patterns in the price movements of markets. Elliott proposed that there are naturally occurring impulsive phases, and then corrective waves grouped in sets of three and five.

Although Elliott is a widely used tool, like many tools and techniques it has its drawbacks. Personally, the major challenge I find is in its complexity, especially for newer traders. People who practise it for a long time, however, can end up mastering it.

I've spent a lot of time breaking down this technique, and I have tried to simplify the concept as it can become confusing and difficult to master.

Whilst I am not here to argue for or against Elliott, I want to explain where I use it and why. I don't want to go into the corrective patterns and have no interest in spending ages scouring the price chart for fractals within fractals except to get a feel for a larger picture. For me, it's a bias. I can get a monthly, weekly and daily direction to help with my directional bias on the bigger picture.

If you want to go off and learn the ins and outs of Elliott, be my guest. I'll even touch on some of the simplified rules later on. But for me, it's a simple directional bias tool.

**'An investor without investment objectives is like a traveller without a destination.'**

**Ralph Seger**

## GANN THEORY

Gann fans, boxes and squares are highly regarded in the industry and, again, are used by many people. I have written several articles on the use of Gann tools. However, the purpose of the mention here is to discuss how the emotional and psychological element plays into human nature, human emotions and pattern recognition. Of course, you can use some of this information to your advantage. I'm not going to explain it all here, but whilst Elliott is mainly price-based, Gann included time. Studying both price and time will give a trader more insight.

Although I would not count myself as a Gann trader, I sometimes apply some Gann techniques for some key levels.

## WYCKOFF

Much like Dow, Elliott and Gann, Richard Wyckoff's view of the market was another assessment of human emotions and how people act under certain stresses. Wyckoff identified specific schematics at key levels in the price action, calling them accumulation and distribution areas. He researched the patterns seen within these phases and was able to label events and create a schematic. Which, again, all makes sense, but shows the power of the emotional elements of the humans operating the chart.

Wyckoff had a term for the behaviour: he called it the Composite Man theory.

## THE COMPOSITE MAN

**'All the fluctuations in the market and in all the various stocks should be studied as if they were the result of one man's operations. Let us call him the Composite Man, who, in theory, sits behind the scenes and manipulates the stocks to your disadvantage if you do not understand the game as he plays it; and to your great profit if you do understand it.'**

**Richard Wyckoff**

Wyckoff told his students to try to understand and play the market game as if the Composite Man was a real entity. The Composite Man has an all-knowing formula.

He explained that the Composite Man carefully plans, executes and concludes his campaigns. He already knows the road map.

The Composite Man attracts the public to buy a stock in which he has already accumulated a sizeable number of shares by making many transactions involving a large number of shares – in effect advertising his stock by creating the appearance of a broad market or a market as a whole.

Wyckoff believed that if one could understand the market behaviour of the Composite Man, one could identify many trading and investment opportunities early enough to profit from them.

This is central to understanding retail traders' psychology, institutional traders' (effectively Composite Man) psychology, and ultimately your own psychology.

## SUMMARY

These individuals were operating over 100 years ago. What they and their theories reveal is that, although markets have moved on, the human element of trading really has not. Yes, there are HFT (High-Frequency Trading) bots and algorithms, but most of the market is still operated by humans playing these games. It is for this very reason that Elliott, Wyckoff, Dow and Gann are still popular today in terms of technical analysis.

You can see why the emotional and psychological ideas remain the same, even after 100 years. Humans are not likely to change their fundamental behavioural patterns any time soon. We are all driven by fear, greed, stupidity, anger – so much so that some commentators have argued that we are pre-programmed to lose when it comes to the financial markets. However, don't despair: knowing this is an edge in its own right.

'DO NOT ANTICIPATE AND MOVE WITHOUT MARKET CONFIRMATION – BEING A LITTLE LATE IN YOUR TRADE IS YOUR INSURANCE THAT YOU ARE RIGHT OR WRONG.'

JESSE LIVERMORE

## Chapter 11

# GETTING INTO PRICE ACTION

## AVOID OVER-COMPLICATING THINGS

I often see new traders over-complicating every aspect of what they do. They will add lines here, there and everywhere. They will fire up 15 indicators to accompany the lines and still end up getting the trade wrong. Some education channels and mentors will give you a preset tactic or strategy, but trading is not a one-size-fits-all type of game. If preset strategies worked, then we'd all be rich. It takes skill to pick out the right opportunities. So, with that being said, where do you start?

Strip it back to the basics, all the way to the simplest of logic. You are trying to make money in a market that can move either up, down or sideways for a short time or over a very long period. So, what if I start by identifying a bias? By bias, I mean a direction I think it is travelling in. At this stage, I do not even care as to where exactly you are in the cycle. I am simply looking for 'up' or 'down'.

When looking at this big picture, it's clear the monthly trend is down (shown by the black line pointing down). The weekly or daily may be up, but the monthly is certainly down at the moment.

This is what I need to start my analysis. Now that I know the monthly move is down, I have a starting point.

Given this information, I am now looking for opportunities to go short (i.e. to make money from the declining price of a stock). I am not trying to catch the bottom and buy. I am simply looking for a continuation of a trend that has lasted several years in this one example. For those of you trading on shorter time frames, you simply use the weekly or daily chart to do the same analysis.

Now you know which direction you aim to go and want a better trade than a 2:1 reward to risk. Simply put, you are making the trade more probable and tipping the odds in your favour.

## PRICE ACTION

Some people will tell you that it's easy enough to use a naked chart, and I agree with this approach, but what about all the tools and indicators? Surely some of them can give you a little more edge. Well, much like the previous chapters, the issue is often what to select and what to reject. Let's start without any and see how much you can get just from the price action itself.

This may sound weird to a new trader. If you are new, you will try new tools and indicators, always looking for something new and shiny. As you know by now, part of my methodology is to strip it back and keep the bare minimum of useful tools. That way, you are not over-burdened with input and confused by multiple signals, so your decision-making ability remains intact.

In this particular example, you already know price action is in a downtrend.

Price action has given you that. You don't need a 200 EMA.

You can safely say you have made an informed decision on the direction you would like to trade.

## CANDLESTICK FORMATIONS

The story goes that early candlestick formations were developed by a Japanese trader called Munehisa Homma to analyse the price of rice contracts. They were brought into Western trading through Steve Nison, who wrote the book *Japanese Candlestick Charting Techniques*, published in 1991.

Many other people have written entire books on price action and the events inside a candle. I could go into depth on countless candlestick formations, what they mean and how to trade them. However, trust me, you don't need all of that either: you just need the bare bones.

When looking at price action, you can identify simple transactions in each and every candle. If a candle is green, it's bullish. If it is red, then it's bearish.

In this example, you have a standard green (bullish) candle – shown here as light grey – that shows the open, high, low and close. If the candle was red (bearish), the close and open would be inverse to the green: the open would be up high and the close down near the bottom.

Candles give some valuable information when you learn to use them. For example, if a candle has a long wick up above and a narrow body, it would suggest buyers have tried to push the price up and failed, with the price closing all the way back down near the open.

Think of a soccer match. The game can be played in each opponent's half for the duration of the game. The game ends at the final whistle, and in terms of the candle, the final whistle is the close. During the game, time was spent in the buying half, and time was spent in the selling half. But it's the final score that counts.

Here is a simple example of some clues you can take from the individual candle.

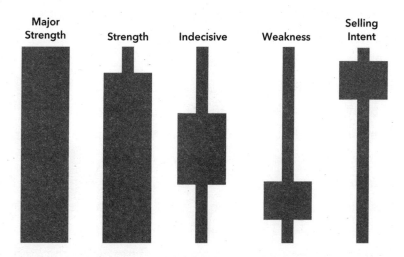

Let's start with the first candle on the left. Why is this major strength? Well, at the end of the match, the bulls were 100% in control. If this candle was red (or dark grey in this case) and wickless, it would suggest bears won that match comprehensively.

Second candle: Although there was a win for the bulls here, the selling pressure near the top means sellers were active and pushing the price back down.

Third candle: Indecision is caused as both ends have wicks, suggesting bears tried to push down and failed, bulls tried to push up and also failed. Now, in simple terms, we could say there is still a little bullish strength here as the candle closed green (light grey), but it's not a convincing win for the bulls. It's this simple logic you want to follow when assessing the candles.

Fourth candle: Why is this weakness on a green (light grey) and bullish candle? At some point in the match, the bears had driven the price all the way from the candle high to very near the candle bottom and closed out. So, although there was intent to push higher, it wasn't enough to close out like candles one or two. This often happens at the end of an uptrend or sometimes in the middle of a trend when a pullback starts.

Fifth candle: The opposite of candle four. This shows sellers have tried to lower the price and failed. You often see this at the bottom of a move before a candle similar to candles one or two pushes the price back up.

Candles are no different from anything else on a chart; the longer the time frame, the more significance you can read into the patterns above. This is especially true of things like stocks and futures, where there is a daily close. This makes the kind of patterns described above more significant.

Just as in the previous chapter – and in this entire book, I am keeping things simple. You don't need it all, and I don't want to waste words where they are not needed. There are a lot of combination candlestick formations, and I'm covering just the ones I think are important.

Candlestick formations can be useful and used on any time frame, though, as stated above, the longer the time frame, the more significant and respectful they become. Just like the individual candles, you need to think of the story the formations are trying to hint towards. Are they forming around significant price levels, older support or resistance, or areas that might be creating a double top or double bottom?

Let's say you get an engulfing candle. This is where the current candle is larger than the candle before it.

The image here shows the circled green candle, in light grey, engulfing the smaller red candle, in dark grey.

The suggestion would be that the trend is likely to start a move up. The logic for this is simple: a lack of selling interest in the small red candle followed by bullish strength in the next large green candle, thus engulfing the smaller candle. The inverse would be true in an uptrend – a smaller green candle being consumed by a larger red candle. You would then expect the next move to be down.

A lot of single candles are regarded as candlestick formations. And truth be told, it's all down to logic. What is the candle trying to tell you?

If you look at what is known as an inside bar, similar to the engulfing candle example – this time you are looking for a candle that has its body and wicks, smaller than the candle before it.

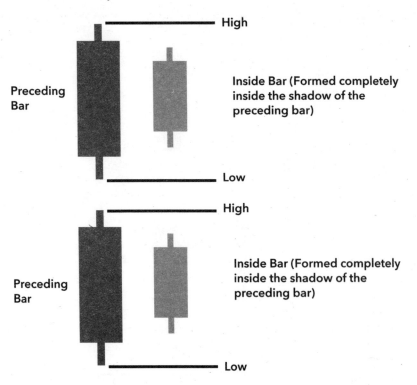

Here's a simple way to see it: my son remembers this by visualising a larger fish swallowing a smaller fish.

Engulfing candles can be another form of indecision. Some trading techniques will teach you to buy on the move above the high of the larger candle and, of course, sell the low. The market has taken a breather, basically, and will likely resume its move or start a new one on the next candle or two. You will sometimes find this to be the start of a range, and the next couple of bars may stay inside the high and low range of that first candle. This is known as a 'contraction'. There will be more on contractions later.

One thing to keep in mind when reading candles or candle formations is that the move after does not need to be immediate. It is like a signal – the suggestion of something 'potentially' about to happen.

'I'M ONLY RICH BECAUSE I KNOW WHEN I'M WRONG. I BASICALLY HAVE SURVIVED BY RECOGNIZING MY MISTAKES.'

GEORGE SOROS

# Chapter 12

# TREND LINES AND CHANNELS

## TREND LINE APPLICATION

There are several ways to apply trend lines to your charts. Some people will tell you that each trend line needs to have two touches to the plotted points; others say three touches. This is an example of people stressing about the wrong things. In fact, trend lines are just another psychological-level tool. My way of drawing them is to find the swing low in an uptrend and anchor the trend line start. Then I extend that out and drag it up until it touches a candle's low.

Step 1:

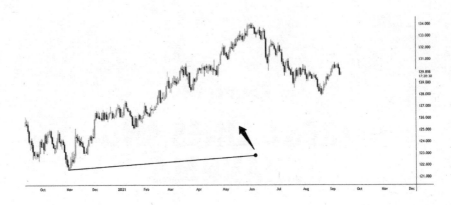

Step 2:

In the image above, you will notice that you get a subsequent touching candle, then the trend gets broken. After the trend-line break, the price then drops and goes back to test the same trend line from below, and then starts making a downward trend.

Downtrend:

Instead of the swing low, you use the same anchor technique but from a swing high instead.

## CHANNELS

The next stage of evolution for trend lines is using two trend lines, forming a channel. There are many types of channels, and they can be applied in various ways.

Let's start with a basic channel that will give us support and resistance.

The upper trend line marks resistance, and the lower trend line marks support. So, both the tops and bottoms of channels represent potential areas of support or resistance.

Trend channels with a negative slope (down) are considered bearish, and those with a positive slope (up) are considered bullish.

Bollinger Bands are also a type of channel, even though they are not drawn as simple trends. As such, the same principles apply (within reason). You'll find they are simply another method for finding psychological support and resistance levels.

Like many elements of trading, these channels can be somewhat subjective, but retail traders will place a lot, if not too much, emphasis on these types of patterns. I tend to use them to help analyse other price actions, rather than as guides to trading in themselves.

With the Elliott Wave Theory, you will see patterns that are formed using wave counts to create ascending/descending channels or contracting and expanding corrective channels. There are more rules in the Elliott application on channels, but the core principles remain the same.

Essentially, what you are looking for is potential areas of rejection or projection equal to spotting support and resistance.

## TREND LINES AND CHANNELS

Here are a couple of bullish examples of channels:

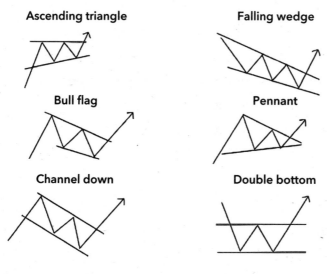

Here are some examples of bearish channels:

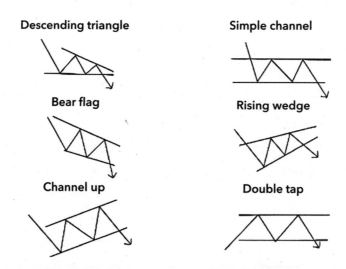

Pitchfork Indicators can also be deemed as channels of sorts, as can Kennedy channels, which have some Elliott Wave applications as well. (I will deal with Kennedy in the Elliott Theory section.)

## WHAT IS A LINEAR REGRESSION CHANNEL?

A linear regression channel is a three-line technical indicator, which outlines the high trend line (the upper line), the low trend line (the lower line), and the middle (median line) of a trend or price move being analysed. The indicator was developed by Gilbert Raff and is often referred to as the Raff Regression Channel (RRC). The linear regression indicator is typically used to analyse the upper and lower limits of an existing trend.

On many trading platforms, you will find automated tools to apply regression channels to your charts.

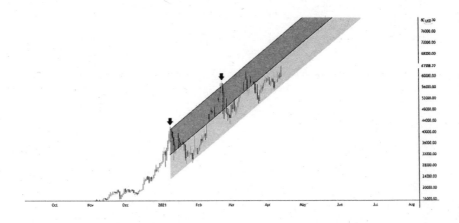

This image shows an automated regression channel being applied. In this example, I have anchored the regression start from the first swing high and dragged it out like a trend line to the second point marked on the chart. The software has then drawn the levels and created the channel.

## INTERESTING LEVELS

What do I mean by interesting (key) levels? These are areas of interest where you can expect something to happen. It might be a bounce in a down move or an area to which price will be magnetically attracted. The importance of these levels depends on the strategy and techniques you want to deploy.

Many new traders are taught about trend lines, moving averages and, of course, supply and demand. Although none of these are technically wrong, and supply and demand are certainly related to (but definitely not the same as) key levels, it all brings us back to the same old point, which is: 'Why do retail traders lose more than they make?'

Trading is a game. You need to train your mind to have a contrarian view compared to the majority of the market. Key levels for retail are hunting grounds for professional traders. Having an imaginary line drawn from two subjective points does not mean you can then go and call this support below and resistance above. Following moving averages up in a trend and calling the average support every time price touches it makes sense only because it seems to work sometimes. Most touches on, say, the 200 EMA, can actually be explained by other previous price action that is less obvious to the untrained eye, so it just appears to be a good guide when in reality it is nothing more than a confusing factor.

When reading financial articles from reputable traders and investors, you will notice they often refer to trend lines and moving averages in ways like 'acting as support/resistance'. This is due to the mind games being played by the big players. Retail traders' emotions are being tested. You need to stop reacting to these like a retail trader and start to see them for the red herrings that they can be. The same applies to highs and lows. You will often notice the price nears a top or a bottom and then pokes its head only a handful of points beyond this before reversing.

## WHY DOES IT DO THIS?

The logic here is a simple one to explain. The big players know that retail have their stops 5, 10 or 15 pips above or below these levels. On a moving average following an uptrend, you will often find a long down-wick on a candle near the moving average line, low enough to make retail think the trend is changing. Stop losses placed by long traders go off, making it fall even more, and this encourages new shorts, which are then cleaned out by the upward trend restarting.

So, how do you use this revelation to help the analysis?

You need to identify the 'real' key levels, which are usually (but not always) unrelated to trend lines and moving averages. There are several ways to spot these, and one of my personal favourites is to use Elliott Waves, but I'll cover this in more detail later. They are a great way to get rough target zones and levels for the longer-term price moves.

This technique is known as 'order blocks' and 'liquidity pools'. You will often hear 'smart-money' traders talk about these. In essence, they are simply areas where you have seen indecision or reversal action previously.

Here is a quick example.

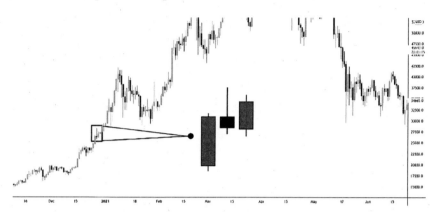

In this picture, you will see that there was a single red weakness candle during a strong uptrend, and then the price carried on up. Without digging too deeply into this, it basically means that there was some interest to sell at these levels that was overridden by buyers.

This means that this level is likely to be tested again to check if there is serious interest in shortening this price point.

Personally, I prefer this type of pattern at swing highs and lows. I often refer to these as the 'buy before a sell' or a 'sell before a buy'.

Although the concept is identical, the location is specific.

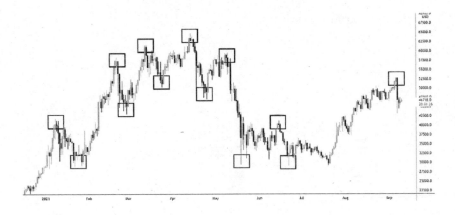

This shows swing highs and lows on the chart – highlighted with boxes. When zoomed in, you would be able to see the buy-before-sell and sell-before-buy candle formations.

All I am looking for here is the last candle of the trend before its reversal. So, when the price is falling then reverses up, I am looking for the last red candle before the move up – almost as if it is the candle that causes the move.

Some smart-money traders will use the candle's body to give them the level. Others will use the whole candle. There is no wrong or right; you can back-test and forward-test this. The instrument will make a difference, as well as the time frame and all kinds of factors. The idea is that you now know where to look.

While the ones that are in the middle of the move are still useful, like the first example, I personally prefer the 'buy before you sell' and 'sell before you buy' moves. Patterns like these can be used on all time frames.

Another technique using this methodology is to draw a line at the 50% marker of the box, and from there it will act as support or resistance later on. Again, the longer the time frame, the more powerful the attraction.

This chart is the same as the first, but I have concentrated on the first box. I use the mid-point of each candle and draw a horizontal ray from there. I have used the full candle for this example, and the instrument is live Bitcoin, so you can see it has not been hand-selected.

The first level acts as resistance before the price drops and creates a new level (box). Then, on its way back up, the price tests and closes on the 50% level of the higher box before breaking through and reaching new highs.

Now, look at the next box of interest.

When the drop came, it was almost exactly to the region of the lower line. Consolidation then happened between both of these levels.

Much like supply/demand and support/resistance, these areas are chasing liquidity. There was two-way interest there before, so the likelihood is that there will be again.

## LIQUIDITY

I've talked about 'interesting areas' – things like the last sell before a buy character change or a candle anomaly in a trending move. Retail traders are often taught about supply/demand as well as support/resistance.

Think of liquidity like an auction house, a place where items are sold in exchange for money, and the auctioneer gets a percentage of the transaction. Now, replace the auctioneer with the broker or exchange. They simply enable a transaction between a buyer and a seller, taking a clip to make it happen.

So, although prices move due to buying and selling, the candles move up and down at every level. However you will notice that every now and again, you get a low or a high and the price reverses. Assume the price is travelling up on the chart towards an arbitrary figure of, say, 100. The price slows as it gets there; it may poke its head just above 100 and make a move down on the next candle back to, say, 90.

Although it's a bit more complex than saying (inaccurately because each seller found a buyer) that it had more sellers than buyers at 100, it's the simplest form of explaining it without too many words that are simply not needed.

Perhaps saying that the sellers were more aggressive than the buyers would better describe it. If you take it as read that there must have been some buyers at 100 as the price did get bid up that far, there weren't many willing to pay more than 100. So, there was more supply than demand at 100.

Although supply and demand are different from support and resistance, you will often see when a price such as our 100 level is rejected. You could now say, 'There was strong resistance at 100, where supply was greater than the demand for the stock/ instrument at this current price.'

Richard Ney likened this to a warehouse. You have to imagine the large operators filling up their shelves before selling to the public. So, when a new trend starts, the warehouse owner will push the sales of products bought at wholesale prices out to retail buyers, who pay retail prices.

If no questions are asked, although the warehouse owner has plenty of stock to fill the demand, he marks it up so that the price rises over time. Although retail traders would like to buy the stock for less, the wholesale prices have been marked up, and you are now buying at the retail level.

Although this is more for accumulation and distribution, the logic remains sound. For the price to move up, there needs to be support often found at key levels, such as the last sell before the buy move sets in. The price will move up as demand increases. The inverse is true in a downtrend, as the price drops: the interest in buying disappears at higher prices, showing the supply is greater than demand at the resistance level.

Having read this book so far, you now know that many new

traders will treat moving averages or imaginary trend lines as support and resistance. What you need to be asking is, do you see supply or demand in or around these levels?

Once a key level is breached, you often see a supply level becoming a demand level later – this is support turning resistance. When you can spot key levels, consolidation clusters and areas of interest, you can simplify your trading approach even further.

## THE MAJOR CONSOLIDATION PATTERN

The major consolidation pattern is a means of using the key levels I've just described. This is categorically not my strategy or technique. You may find it under different names or taught in slightly different ways. But, as in the rest of this book, it's an example of something that I decided was valuable, part of the 10% – a technique that I find useful at times, at key levels.

After a period of consolidation, you often find an expansion phase. This is a sucker's move to trap traders on the wrong side. You will see this in the example below. Once the consolidation and the expansion are completed, you will get a move back to the middle, and, at this point, you will go into a new trend. You will see this pattern play out over and over again.

When you spot these, you can either use them completely on their own to trigger trade ideas or you can use them in conjunction with liquidity levels and 'special areas', such as consolidations at Elliott Wave turning points. The latter gives more confirmation or confluence.

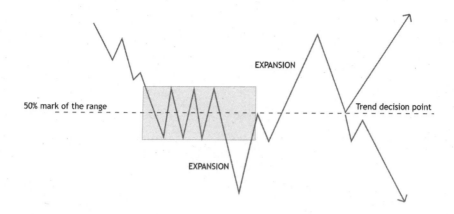

This image shows the concept in line form to simplify the visual concept of each phase.

In the example above, you will often notice that the expansion will be equidistant above and below the consolidation range. A test of the 50% level would be expected, and then the trend will give confirmation either way.

In a later chapter, I'll be talking about Wyckoff Schematics. In a way, this method is similar to a Wyckoff Schematic occurring on a shorter time frame.

Hence, as the consolidation is part of the schematic, its location within the primary trend will often give you a clue as to the direction of the continuation, along with the logic for either a distribution or accumulation at this price level. Flick back to this chapter after reading about Wyckoff later.

'IF YOU WANT SOMETHING YOU'VE NEVER HAD, YOU MUST BE WILLING TO DO SOMETHING YOU'VE NEVER DONE.'

THOMAS JEFFERSON

'TRADE WHAT'S HAPPENING
. . . NOT WHAT YOU THINK
IS GONNA HAPPEN.'
DOUG GREGORY

## Chapter 13

# VOLUME

## VOLUME BASICS

Trading volume is a measure of how much of a given financial asset has traded over a given period. In stocks, volume is measured in the number of shares traded and, for futures and options, it is based on how many contracts have changed hands. For foreign exchange, it is supplied by banks' price feeds, and while it does not comprise the total worldwide volume, it is a broadly representative sample.

This is also true in crypto – although there are other tools available due to blockchain technology, such as on-chain analytics.

The Dow Theory talks about using volume as an indicator. When the price rises and the volume rises as well, it's a good sign of positive momentum. The opposite is also true. If the price is rising, but volume is decreasing, you might see an end or at least a correction in the direction it is currently travelling.

In short, volume can help highlight the strength of a trend and spot anomalies between the volume and the price action.

In this example, you can see increasing volume to the upside as the market rallied. This shows buying strength.

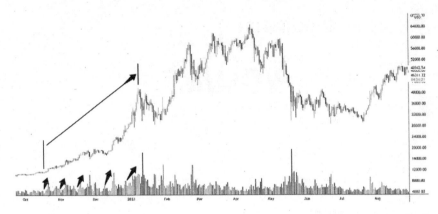

However, when you start to see decreasing volume as the price moves up, you can identify a type of divergence, as seen in this chart.

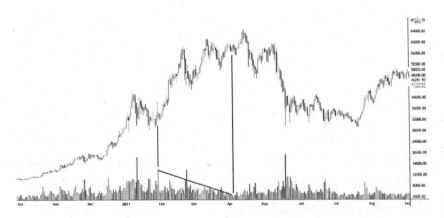

So, whereas a rise in volume indicates strength in the move, declining or unchanged volume on a breakout indicates a lack of interest and a higher probability of a fake breakout.

## VOLUME

Most traders fail to realise there are other methods of seeing the same data, such as On-Balance Volume (OBV), Chaikin Money Flow and Weis Waves.

## ON-BALANCE VOLUME (OBV)

OBV is a simple but effective indicator. Volume is added, starting with an arbitrary number, when the market finishes higher, or volume is subtracted when the market finishes lower. This provides a running total and shows which stocks are being accumulated. It can also show divergences, such as when a price rises but volume increases at a slower rate or even begins to fall.

## CHAIKIN MONEY FLOW

Rising prices should be accompanied by rising volume. Chaikin Money Flow focuses on measuring volume when prices finish in the upper or lower portion of their daily range and then provides a value for the corresponding strength. When closing prices are in the upper portion of the day's range and volume is expanding, the values will be positive. When closing prices are in the lower portion of the range, values will be negative. It is a bit like OBV and can be used as a short-term indicator because it oscillates, but, like OBV, it is more commonly used for seeing divergences.

## WEIS WAVES

The Weis Wave is an adaptation of Wyckoff's method designed for use in today's volatile markets. It works in all time periods and can be applied to the futures, forex, stock, crypto and commodity markets.

The Weis Wave first takes the market volume and then organises it with the price into wave charts, often depicted in a type of oscillator below the candles or bars of the main chart.

I use Weis more for the larger waves; it is a very quick and accurate way to identify third waves in an Elliott Wave count.

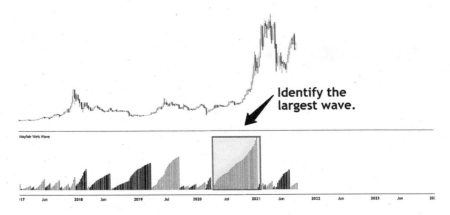

Identify the largest wave.

The Weis Wave is an adaptation of Wyckoff's method that handles today's volatile markets.

In the image above, I have simplified the waves and identified Wave 3 first. If you then look closer, you will notice a move 0-1 equals impulsive, 2 is a corrective which is shown on the Weis indicator as red, green, red, green, then red. Then the main move

## VOLUME

3 starts – a very simple technique but very effective to assist with Elliott Wave logic.

There have been many books on volume, strategies and techniques, but what I am trying to give here is a summary of how to simplify your trading to such a degree that it becomes obvious. This Weis technique will build your confidence when counting the Elliott Wave sequences.

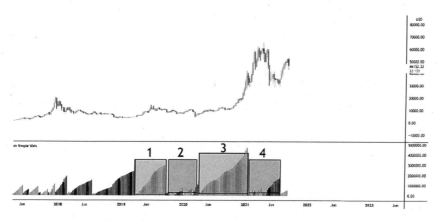

'ONE OF THE FUNNY THINGS ABOUT THE STOCK MARKET IS THAT EVERY TIME ONE PERSON BUYS, ANOTHER SELLS, AND BOTH THINK THEY ARE ASTUTE.'

*WILLIAM FEATHER*

# Chapter 14

# VOLUME PROFILES

Volume profiles attempt to analyse what volume traded at what price.

There are several ways to add volume profiles to your chart. They include:

- Fixed range volume
- Session volume
- Visible range volume

They all work pretty much the same way, but you need to be careful when assessing visible range volume profiles because zooming in and out would be of little use and probably lead to confusion.

Session volume can be useful, and you can dig down a layer or two deeper than this by going into the delta view, footprint and depth of market (DOM) views.

A volume profile is a horizontal histogram plotted on a security's chart, showing the volume of shares traded at a specific price level. Often, price volume histograms are found on the Y-axis and are used by traders to predict areas of support and resistance. In comparison, the simple volume display shows the volume inside each bar on the X-axis.

Volume profiles illustrate high buying and selling interest at specific price levels. The area with the highest volume is called the value range. The value range is often set as standard to 70% of the whole range, meaning 70% of the volume traded within it. In addition to this, when you notice relatively high-volume bars, you can narrow the focus down to what is known as the point of control (POC). The best way to visualise this is to think of it as an auction. The point of control will be the main auction area, acting as large-scale support and resistance.

As well as the POC and the value range, you will have histogram bars with more volume than others but less than the POC; you would expect these to act as weaker support and resistance. You then have low-volume bars on the histogram. These indicate levels that are likely to see the price shoot quickly through them to the next level with higher volume.

The logic behind this is simple. At higher-volume areas, there are more buyers and sellers active.

It's important to note that price-by-volume charts show total volume at certain price levels over a period of time. So, if a session volume profile is selected, the data will be representing data day by day, while a fixed range volume will display the data histogram for the full range you select. This can be useful for looking at specific price action formations.

Any data outside the range is ignored, so the projected support and resistance levels in the future might be less helpful if you haven't selected the right range.

In the example below, I took a fixed-range volume profile and applied it from the swing high – in this case, the all-time high (ATH) of Bitcoin at the time of writing.

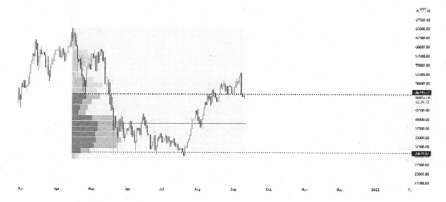

You will see the value range highlighted by the dotted lines and the POC highlighted by the dark grey line. This shows that most of the trading activity since the major drop has been between these levels, and the later rally attracted relatively little volume.

Although a little harder to see in a book, the session volume on shorter time frames gives you the exact same data for each 24-hour period or session.

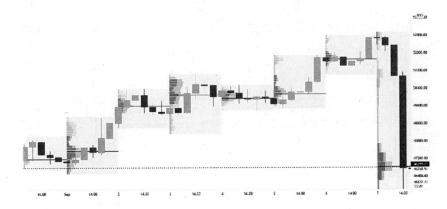

There are four common shapes you see over and over again when using volume:

## P-SHAPED PROFILES

A P-shaped volume profile typically occurs when a market rises sharply and then consolidates. Once the price reaches the upper end of a P-shaped profile, there may be a period of consolidation where equilibrium is struck between buyers and sellers. The lower part of a P-shaped profile is long and thin, which represents a low volume release. The larger top section represents where a 'fair' price has been achieved and trading activity has been high. P-shaped patterns can be interpreted as bullish signals.

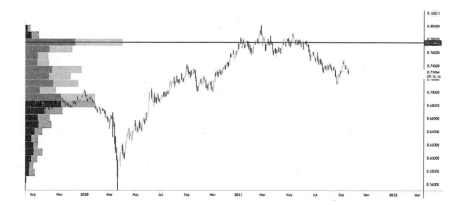

Above you will see the lighter levels are the heavier volume, and the darker lower areas of volume. Using this logic, you can paint a '**P**' as shown in the image below. This method applies to the other shapes 'b', 'D' and 'B'.

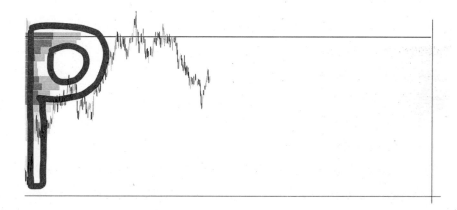

## B-SHAPED PROFILES

A b-shaped volume profile is formed when a market falls sharply and then consolidates. In contrast to a P-shaped profile, a b-shaped volume profile can occur following a long wind-up.

While P-shaped profiles represent short coverage, b-shaped

profiles represent a period of selling before equilibrium is found in a market. The top of a b-shaped profile is long and thin, representing low volume and an 'unfair' perception of price. The wider lower section represents where the price has again struck a balance between buyers and sellers. A b-shaped profile is commonly found during downtrends, but when the b-shape is seen during an uptrend, it can potentially indicate a reversal. Since the b-shaped profiles represent longs exiting the market, they are generally viewed as bearish.

## D-SHAPED PROFILES

D-shaped profiles occur when there is a temporary equilibrium in a market. The POC is usually located in the centre of the profile, indicating a balance between buyers and sellers. Neither the buyers nor the sellers were more aggressive. However, patient order flow traders may look for D-shaped volume profiles in anticipation of a possible two-way breakout as institutional players strengthen their positions.

## CAPITAL B-SHAPED PROFILES

A capital B-shaped volume profile may be observed when two D-shaped profiles occur within a specified period. Although there is only one value area and one POC, some order flow traders will split the profile into two distinct D areas with their own value areas. While the capital B-shaped profiles are generally interpreted as the continuation of a trend, it is important to note which POC is more dominant – indicating whether activity was highest at the top or bottom of the profile.

Here's a little trick to spot volume clusters without the tools. It can be very useful to train your eye into seeing these on a naked chart.

First of all, draw the levels as a rectangle in all of the 'congestion' zones where there is a fair amount of price action. These are, in essence, the auction areas.

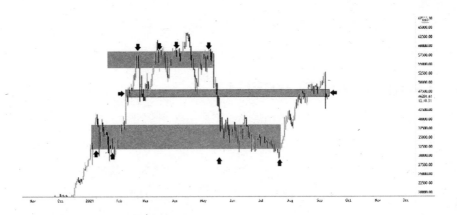

Next, try to spot the area with the most activity. This is easily done by assessing the size of the box and secondly how many times the price interacted in these zones.

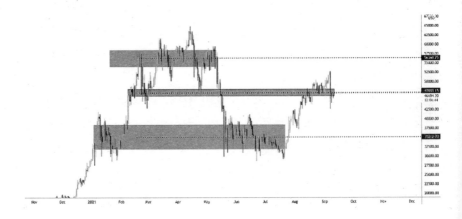

So, as I look at the three zones in descending order, I would have to say the bottom box has the heaviest traffic, followed by the top box, which is narrower, and then finally the middle box. Based on this, my assumption would be strong support resistance in the middle and the point of control down towards the centre of the bottom box. Finally, strong resistance is expected at the level of the top box.

Let's apply the fixed range.

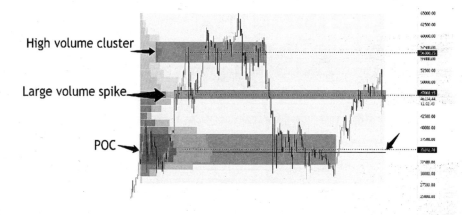

There are various techniques for using volume. There are even strategies purely based on volume, but the purpose here is to give you an introduction and breakdown of how it works and what is behind it, along with how you can compute it without even drawing it.

Now that you have this knowledge, you can apply it when you look at forecasted Fibonacci levels, for example, maybe even using these levels to tighten up stops, suggest exits, or entries for a trade.

## MARKET FOOTPRINT, DEPTH OF MARKET AND DELTA

Expanding on volume and volume profile, the next degree of knowledge is to see not only inside the volume but the volume inside the candles.

The footprint, depth of market (DOM) and the delta go hand in hand.

Footprint charts are basically a type of candlestick chart that provides additional information, such as trade volume and order flow, in addition to the price. This takes the analysis beyond just the security's price. This tool is a unique offering that is gaining popularity among leading charting software providers.

Order flow and DOM mostly contain the same information, but they have different ways of representing it. In layman's terms, the order flow/DOM is the representation of the orders on the book. DOM is the measure of the supply and demand for liquid, tradable assets. It is based on the number of open buy and sell orders for a given asset, such as a stock or futures contract. The greater the quantity of those orders, the deeper or more liquid the market.

This data is also known as the order book since it consists of a list of pending orders for a security or currency. The data in the book is used to determine which transactions can be processed or how much total volume could be bought or sold by pushing up or down through the order book to a certain price.

Depth of market is often displayed as an electronic list of outstanding buys and sell orders, organised by price level and updated in real time to reflect current activity. A matching engine pairs up compatible trades for completion.

The delta footprint displays the net difference at each price between the volume initiated by buyers and the volume initiated by sellers. The delta footprint helps traders confirm that a price trend has started and will continue.

So, in summary, it is showing you inside the candle – the number of orders, the types of orders and so on. When combining all three aspects, you have a view of the orders, their type and the difference. This can be useful for shorter scalp-type trades as it would give a slight edge over the more traditional candles and line charts.

Below is an example of a footprint chart with the delta at the bottom.

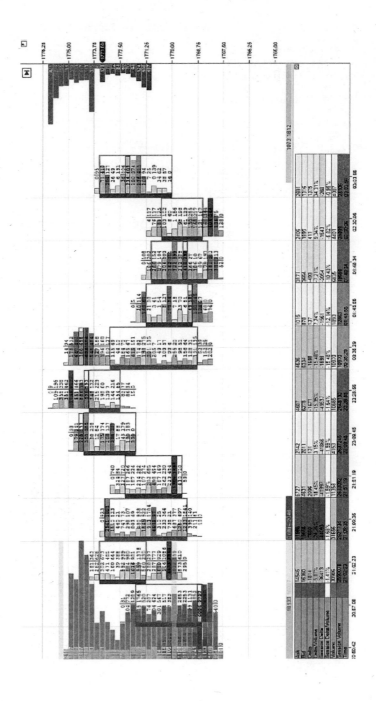

# VOLUME PROFILES

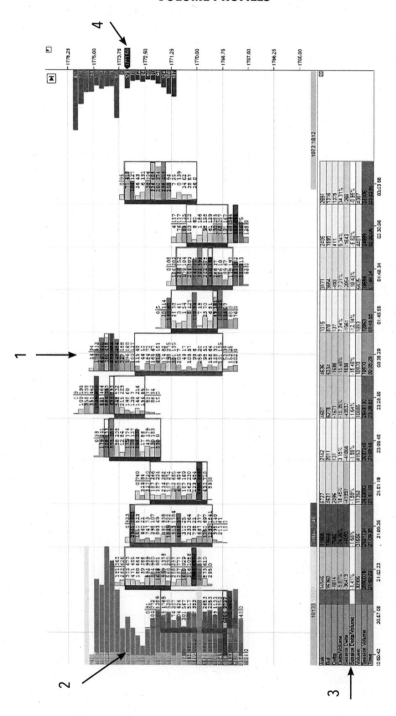

147

I have labelled the chart from the previous page to give you some insight into what you are seeing. You will notice numbers next to the candles, but you will see the candles themselves are still red and green (dark grey and light grey).

The numbers are known as order flow or footprint. This shows the order book of positions at the price level. How many buyers and sellers, in essence.

Volume profile as covered at the start of this chapter.

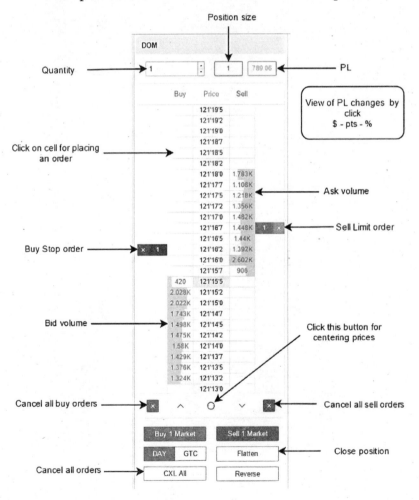

# VOLUME PROFILES

This is the cumulative delta. It is the difference between buying and selling power. Volume delta is calculated by taking the difference between the volume traded at the offer price and the volume traded at the bid price.

A variation on what's known as depth of market (DOM). This shows the levels of a particular instrument that are being traded at different prices. This allows traders to understand the supply and demand, and therefore liquidity of the currency at each price point. A good depth of market means that there will be good liquidity.

'THE BIG MONEY IS NOT IN THE BUYING OR THE SELLING, BUT IN THE WAITING.'

CHARLIE MUNGER

# Chapter 15

# DOW THEORY

We previously looked at Dow Theory, briefly, in Chapter 10. Now let's approach it in more detail.

I think of the Dow Theory as the logic for taking a trade. Let's look at it methodically. First of all, you are looking for the primary trend. For me, this means looking at the monthly chart.

Now you are looking for the secondary trend, so I would use the weekly chart for this.

As you can see from the chart, you are making lower lows and lower highs – as expected, given the longer time frame. The trend is down.

As we start to drill down into what I call the 'road map', the secondary trend swing lows or highs are good starting points to take shorter-time-frame trades. Ideally, you would prefer to take a trade that has a lot of confluence between the primary, secondary and smaller trends (i.e. they are all in the same direction). In one very logical step, we just increased our odds of a successful trade. How easy was that?

The concept of the road map is important. We can take where we are on the journey and then apply other techniques, such as Elliott and Wyckoff, with more accuracy because we know where we are on the overall route.

Knowing where we are on the road map at any given time can create an incredibly accurate bias.

# DOW THEORY

Dow's second tenet is that we have three phases: the accumulation, the distribution and the trending phase, which can be in either direction. The majority of the time, the market is going sideways.

You can now use the information gained by applying Dow Theory, as described above, to determine whether or not we are accumulating, distributing or in the trending move.

Using the same example, you can identify phases that can then be assessed on shorter time frames.

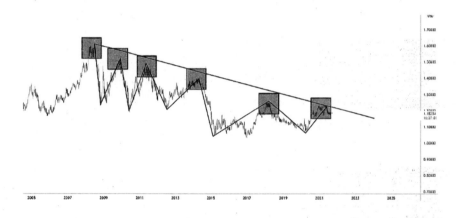

Moving in fractally, on shorter time frames, you will spot distribution happening at these boxes.

At the lows, you can see the accumulation phases.

The beauty of this is that you are now starting to narrow down the options for the trade entry. If you determine our bias (direction), it becomes easier to figure out the phase it is in. We are increasing your odds at every stage.

Dow's third tenet is that news discounts everything. By this, he meant price action is king, and all information in the news has already been assessed by the larger operators. This means, in the

155

overall trend, it is far less important than you may think. The news causes interference and noise in shorter time frames, so it is more significant, but it is extremely easy to allow the news to confuse you rather than assist you in trading. If you learn to regard news more as a risk than a helper, then you will be better off.

The fourth tenet is that stock market averages must confirm each other. I feel this is less relevant in non-equity instruments, but when trading forex, commodities or crypto, the US Dollar Index (DXY) is a great tool to confirm directional bias because most instruments are priced against the dollar, meaning the dollar is the currency of exchange. When buying gold or oil, even Bitcoin, it's all done via transactions to and from the dollar.

This means that a strong dollar will soften the other instrument. To explain this, as the dollar rises, you need fewer dollars to buy whatever the instrument is, so the price falls. In summary, when the dollar is rising, you would expect oil, gold, Euro and Bitcoin to drop. Whilst it's not as simple as this, the direction or bias you have in DXY will always be a good indication.

Dow's fifth tenet is that increasing volume confirms the trend.

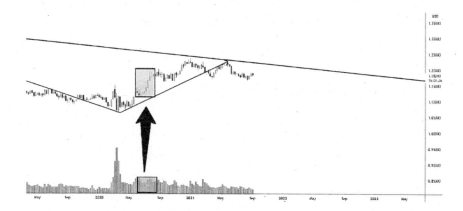

In the example above, you will see a large red spike in volume. From this low, you start to see the secondary trend moving up. This is confirmed with volume increasing as the move goes up.

If you are seeing volume decreasing but the price rising, it's a good indication there is something untoward with the move, and a trend change could be imminent.

The sixth tenet states that the trend continues until a definitive signal confirms otherwise. A break of a trend line is a good example.

The Dow Theory is simple, yet most technical analysis fits inside it.

As you will get to see later, when you combine Dow with Elliott and Wyckoff techniques, you can quickly get an overall bias on the longer time frames, plus you can identify trend phases that will aid you in your decision-making. Without the use of indicators, you can focus on price action.

Indicators can and sometimes do add confluence. However, more often than not, people get confused by trying to cover every single aspect. I often see people with 15 indicators on their chart, most of which say the same thing in different colours or styles. As before, keep it simple.

**'Investing is the intersection of economics and psychology.'**

**Seth Klarman**

When thinking about technical analysis, I often visualise the logic as a family tree. Where the Dow Theory covers the broad spectrum, the work carried out by Elliott, Wyckoff and Gann drilled deeper into the core values and theories described by the former.

In the later chapters, which cover Elliott, Wyckoff and Gann in depth, you will see the puzzle come together and how the technical analysis techniques can work hand in hand to create a winning strategy.

# Chapter 16

# FIBONACCI

Leonardo Fibonacci, also known as Leonardo Bonacci or Leonardo of Pisa, was an Italian mathematician from the Republic of Pisa, considered to be 'the most talented Western mathematician of the Middle Ages'.

Fibonacci popularised the Hindu-Arabic numeral system in the Western world, primarily through his composition in 1202 of *Liber Abaci* (Book of Calculation). He also introduced Europe to the sequence of Fibonacci numbers.

The Fibonacci numbers, commonly denoted Fn, form a sequence called the Fibonacci sequence, such that each number is the sum of the two preceding ones, starting from 0 and 1:

0–1–1–2–3–5–8–13–21–34 etc.

He noticed this pattern popping up in nature spontaneously.

You may have already seen this diagram.

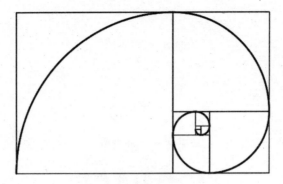

This is the Fibonacci Golden Ratio Spiral, made up of the Fibonacci sequence of numbers; another technique used by many traders, beyond Fibonacci extensions and retracements.

Fibonacci is quite simply all about ratios; the sequence of numbers fits into everything from spirals, planet alignment, the human body, sunflowers and even sea shells.

You will see these patterns over and over again. Another famous sketch you will probably be familiar with is Leonardo Da Vinci's famous drawing The Vitruvian Man.

# FIBONACCI

It is the Fibonacci ratio in the human body. If you measure from the floor to the belly button, you get 1, and if you measure from the belly button to the top of your head, you get 0.618, giving you 1.618 total.

How do you use the sequence in trading?

One way of using Fibonacci in trading is to predict the potential targets and/or pullbacks of swings in the trend:

1. The numbers in the sequence have a ratio of 1.618.
2. The inverse of 1.618 is 0.618.
3. There are other numbers that are used in the sequence but are less relevant when predicting extensions. These numbers are: 0.236, 0.382 and 0.786.

Imagine a pullback in an uptrend. How far will it pull back on average? It turns out to be around one of these levels more often than not.

As these are symmetrical when used, they create patterns recognised by the human brain, known as subconscious pattern recognition. When prices near these levels, profits are taken, stops are triggered and new entries are added. This principle you will see over and over again. In the next chapter are some examples of Fibonacci.

'FOUR MOST DANGEROUS WORDS IN THE INVESTMENT WORLD: "THIS TIME IT'S DIFFERENT."'

HEMANT BENIWAL

# Chapter 17

# ELLIOTT WAVE PRINCIPLE

The Elliott Wave principle is again all about psychology, although it is globally recognised as another form of technical analysis.

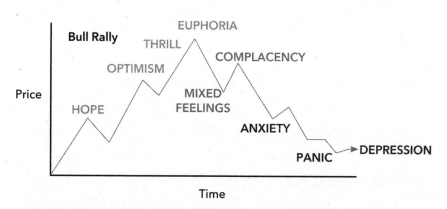

The image above shows the human emotions throughout a bull move. You can start to apply Elliott counts to this.

When applying Elliott, you have some hard rules, although relatively simple. This will allow you to really dumb down the Elliott Wave Theory as a whole.

The same cycle from the previous image is now showing a count in Elliott format below.

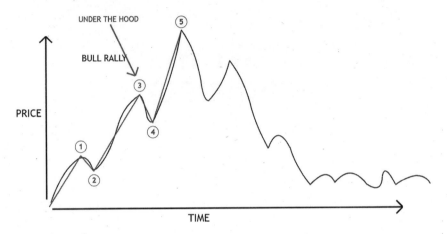

The market cycle will often look like a 5-wave impulsive move (with the trend), followed by a 3-wave corrective move (counter trend). This can be explained in several simple steps. Impulse waves are normally labelled 1-2-3-4-5, and correctives are labelled A-B-C.

There are three major rules that cannot be broken.

1. Wave 2 cannot retrace more than 100% of the first wave.

2. The third wave can never be the shortest of waves 1, 3 and 5.

3. Wave 4 can't go beyond the third wave at any time.

When working with the Elliott Wave principle, you have the major or primary trend (the example above shows an uptrend). This is impulsive (light grey), and then you have the corrective (dark grey) move.

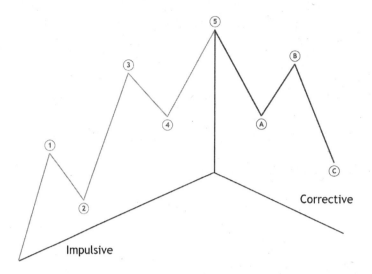

These waves are also fractal, meaning you have mini trends within each wave. For example, you will see five smaller waves from 0-1 and again from 2-3 and then finally from 4-5.

Moves 1-2 and 3-4 are corrective, and just like ABC on the right side of this image, you have corrective smaller waves inside. And if you drop a time frame, you will have waves inside that wave and so on.

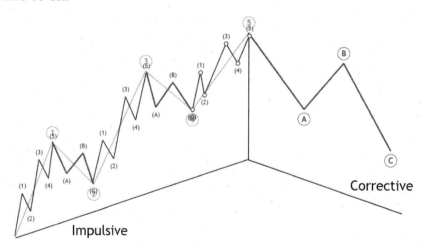

This might seem very confusing at first, but all you need to do is look at the primary trend (as the Dow Theory suggests) and obtain the bias. In an uptrend, you would start a count from the major swing low, and in a downtrend, the count would begin at the major swing high.

> **'Trading doesn't just reveal your character; it also builds it if you stay in the game long enough.'**
> **Yvan Byeajee**

Some additional rules and useful guidance:
- Wave 4 cannot enter the range below the high of wave 1 (in an uptrend).

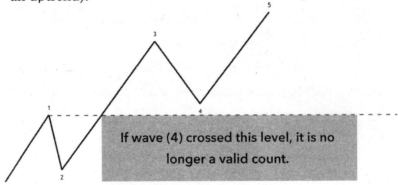

If wave (4) crossed this level, it is no longer a valid count.

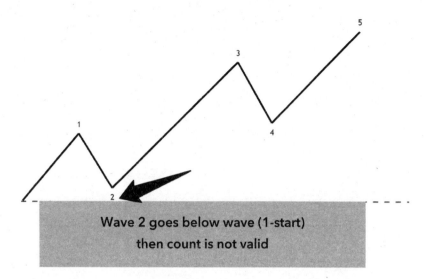

- Wave 1-2 can retrace 99% of wave 0-1, but if it goes lower than the 0, it invalidates the count.

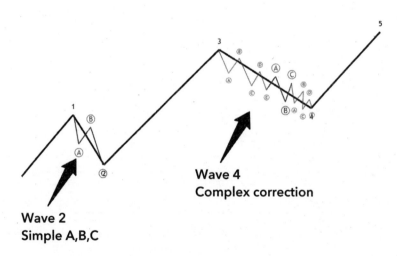

- Waves 1-2 and 3-4 are often opposite, so if 1-2 is a simple ABC, wave 3-4 is likely to be more complex (combo move). The illustration only shows the concept and not an exact count.

- Often, wave 3-4 is shallow in comparison to wave 1-2, often going 38%–61.8% of wave 2-3.

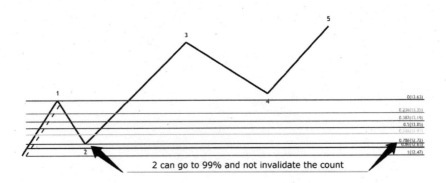

2 can go to 99% and not invalidate the count

But with wave 4, this is often less of a pullback than that of wave 2:

- Often into 38% but sometimes also down to what's known as the 'golden range', which is between 50% and 61.8% (of course, it can go deeper), as long as it does not enter wave 1.

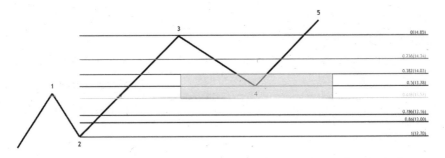

If you use a Fibonacci extension from 0-1 and back to 0, you can mark off the 1.618 and the 2.618, sometimes even the 3.618 or higher. You will see these are common levels for the price to target. You can also use an extension from 0-1 and only back to 2, thus giving a range or a zone.

Here's a textbook example. You shouldn't expect each one to be perfect like this, but this wave is what other Elliott Waves aspire to be.

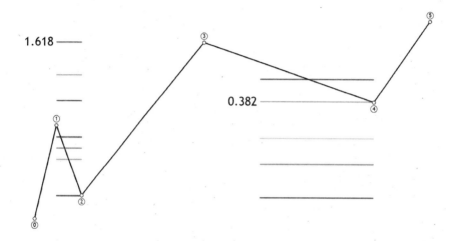

0-1-2 Extension 1.618 gives us 3, then a 0.382 retracement gives you 4. I'm not estimating 5 yet.

1-2 is steep, making it different from 3-4, which is also nice.

To help us be sure, you look inside wave 3 for an internal, or fractal, wave. The shorter the time frame, the less you expect perfection.

You can now take a trade on any wave start. Starting later means having more evidence on hand when it's decision time, but starting earlier offers more reward to risk.

Let's assume you think we are currently in a wave 3-4.

The signs that 4 is in, and it's off to wave 5:

1. It just bounced off or near a recognised retracement level.
2. It made an impulsive move up with a 50%–99% pullback.
3. It is up again after failing to make that new low.
4. You can see at least a simple three-wave move down to complete 4.
5. 4 doesn't look like 2.

Assuming all is well, you now have the ability to look for an entry on the smaller 1-2 pullback move, using a tight stop loss, to enter long. (It's fractal.)

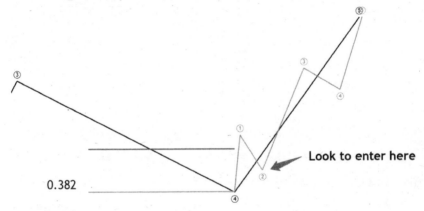

Place the stop loss below the black 4 or below the green 2 if you are sure that 2 is in. This gives some pretty good risk to reward.

How can I quantify my RR?

You know the risk (my SL), but now you need to know the reward. This won't be exact – it's an art more than a science – but you can calculate some ranges.

Rules for wave 4-5:

1. The same price change as wave 1

2. Between 1.273 and 1.618 of 3-4

3. 1.618 of wave 1-3.

These are usually different levels, obviously, but they give you a minimum and a maximum. Here's what the range looks like:

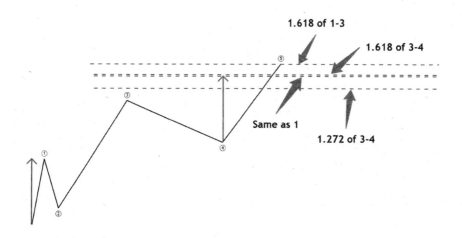

You can get a good idea of the behaviour as it reaches each level and decide for yourself if wave 5 looks like it comprises 5 waves yet.

If you see the candles start to shorten and volume reduction, then it's likely to reverse or at least give an indication a reversal is due. Couple that with the Fibonacci levels and Elliott count, and you will see how they work together.

## KENNEDY CHANNELS

Another little technique that can be useful when applied to Elliott are Kennedy channels named after Jeffrey Kennedy.

Consider this picture:

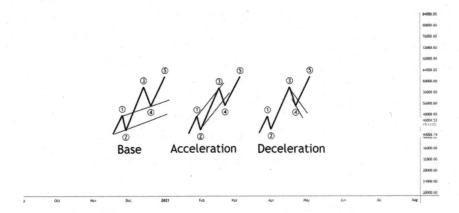

Base channels start at the 0 (zero) point and connect to the low 2. Then a parallel channel is drawn and extended from point 1. The acceleration channel is drawn by connecting the high of waves 1 and 3, and then drawing a parallel channel starting at the low of point 2. These can both help to determine the end of wave 4.

To draw the deceleration channel, start by drawing an A-B-C corrective wave from point 3. Draw a trend line from point 3 to the end of wave B. Take a parallel of this line and place it on the extreme of wave A. Price action that stays within one price channel is often corrective. When prices break through the upper boundary line of this channel, you can expect a fifth-wave rally next.

## ANALYSIS

Base Channels: Prices need to break out of the base channel to confirm the trend.

Acceleration Channels: Movement out of the acceleration channel confirms that wave 4 is in progress.

Deceleration Channels: Penetration of the deceleration channel lines signals that wave 5 is under way.

## ELLIOTT SUMMARY

Although there are more advanced techniques to learn when using Elliott, most have to do with the corrective moves – both bearish and bullish.

The impulsive moves (with the trend) are always five moves. However, corrective moves can be ABC which would be a three-wave move, or they can be more complex and create combinations that come in various forms.

The simple formats are:

1. Zig Zag – An ABC made up like this: A-5 waves, B-3 waves, C-5 waves.

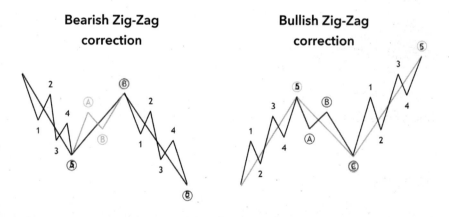

**Bearish Zig-Zag correction**    **Bullish Zig-Zag correction**

You can see the larger main A, B, C in red on the bearish example and green on the bullish example above. The smaller counts are overlaid.

2. Flats – They consist of a 3-3-5 move and come in three variations: regular, expanded and running.

### Regular flat

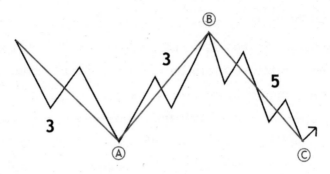

In the image on the previous page, I have highlighted where you will spot the count. From (0) to A, you can see three smaller swings, from A to B, again three smaller swings, and then from B to C, you can see the five smaller swings.

3. Triangles – They consist of a 3-3-3-3-3 move. These come in four types: ascending and descending, contracting and expanding types.

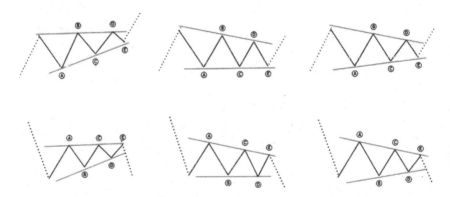

**Ascending, Contracting and Descending**

As you will see from the images above, the terminology matches the type from ascending on the left, contracting in the centre, and descending on the right. The top three are bullish and the bottom three are bearish.

> 4. Double threes and triple threes – a combo of the corrective patterns: zig-zag, flats and triangles.

Wave 2 and wave 4 can be very complex and make it hard to determine where in the process the price is. They can be very profitable; knowing the rules will help you stay in the game.

Personally, these days, I don't trade the 4 due to it being an absolute nightmare, too volatile and not worth the additional time on analysis!

## EXPANDING FLATS

Let's expand a bit on expanding flats (excuse the pun). They comprise a corrective three-wave move labelled as ABC where:

- A and B are constituted of three waves
- A subdivision of waves A and B can be in any corrective three-wave structure including zigzag, flat, double three and triple three
- Wave B of the 3-3-5 pattern terminates beyond the starting level of wave A
- Wave C is five waves, impulse or diagonal
- Wave C ends substantially beyond the ending level of wave A
- Wave C needs to have momentum divergence

- Fibonacci Ratio Relationship:
  - Wave B = 123.6% of wave A.
  - Wave C = 123.6%–161.8% of wave AB.

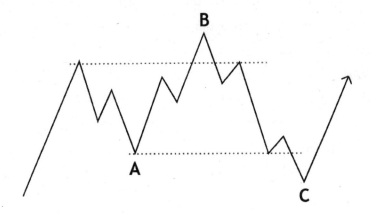

As the image above shows, expanding flats can go beyond the previous high or low to create their B wave.

## SHORTENING OF THE THRUST (SOT)

There are two corrective formations that are worth covering, and they both involve something called the shortening of the thrust. These are leading diagonals and ending diagonals.

Please bear in mind I don't advocate trading in corrective moves, though I do study them still – more like data gathering than to actually trade each sub-wave.

## LEADING DIAGONALS

Although technically bullish, I like to think of leading diagonals more as a hybrid, special type of motive wave, which appears as a subdivision of wave 1 in an impulse or subdivision of wave A in a zigzag.

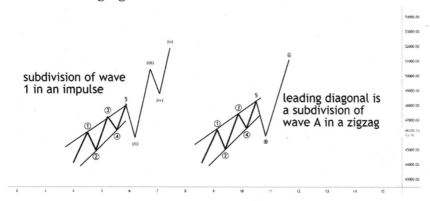

The leading diagonal is a subdivision of wave 1 in an impulse.

The leading diagonal is usually characterised by overlapping waves 1 and 4 and also by the wedge shape. Overlap between waves 1 and 4 is not a condition; it may or may not happen.

The subdivision of a leading diagonal can be 5-3-5-3-5 or 3-3-3-3-3. The examples above show a leading diagonal with 5-3-5-3-5 subdivisions.

## ENDING DIAGONALS

These are a special type of motive wave, which appears as a subdivision of wave 5 in an impulse or subdivision of wave C in a zigzag.

An ending diagonal is usually characterised by overlapping wave 1 and 4; in essence, this is the same as the shortening of the thrust.

The subdivision of an ending diagonal is either 3-3-3-3-3 or 5-3-5-3-5.

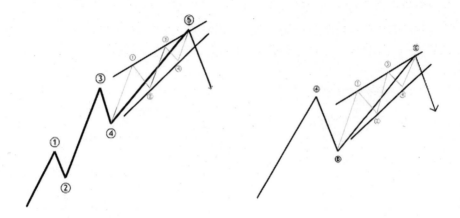

## SOT SUMMARY

A shortening of the thrust usually indicates a change of behaviour in the market by highlighting less and less progress made in the direction of a recent trend. New supply or demand exerts itself, causing the SOT, and this may lead to a pullback or a change in trend, which is the same as the ending diagonals, only different terminology.

## TRADING CORRECTIVES

You can trade corrective waves if you like, but I don't recommend it. I can't stress this enough. Wave 4 is 'designed' to take away all the profit gained in wave 3.

Too many possibilities mean that the Elliott analysis can get very complex and very confusing. Many traders who only utilise Elliott Wave Theory often confuse themselves and over-analyse the market as a whole.

I personally just look for the 1-2 of the 5.

Much like the rest of this book, the idea is to keep it simple.

Once you have a basic grasp of the impulsive 5 move and a basic understanding of the corrective options, you can use Elliott Wave principles to give a bias for your trade direction.

'THERE IS A TIME TO GO
LONG, A TIME TO GO
SHORT, AND A TIME TO GO
FISHING.'

*JESSE LIVERMORE*

# Chapter 18

# WYCKOFF

Wyckoff had a keen eye for price movements. By relentlessly studying price movements – he was one of the first 'tape-readers' – Richard Wyckoff learned that the market is not as chaotic as one would be led to believe.

As mentioned earlier, there are schematics for Wyckoff that can be applied to decipher the smaller moves, and again they can be shown to operate fractally.

Now, let's look inside the Composite Man's logic.

I've already talked about accumulation and distribution in the section about Dow. In Wyckoff, there are two main types of accumulation and two main types of distribution. Often the hardest part of working with Wyckoff's theory is knowing what schematic to look for.

The Dow Theory helps to work this out. By knowing the

primary trend and the immediate situation, you can get a pretty good feel for what to expect given where on the chart we are.

Coupling that with Elliott Waves, you get a pretty clear picture because you can assume that in an uptrend, the points 0, 2 and 4 would be accumulation, and at points 1, 3 and 5, you can expect some form of distribution.

The inverse is true for a downtrend.

I hope you are starting to see how this all fits together, piece by piece.

> **'Investing should be more like watching paint dry or watching grass grow. If you want excitement, take $800 and go to Las Vegas.'**
>
> **Paul Samuelson**

## ACCUMULATION

Schematic 1                    MAYFAIR

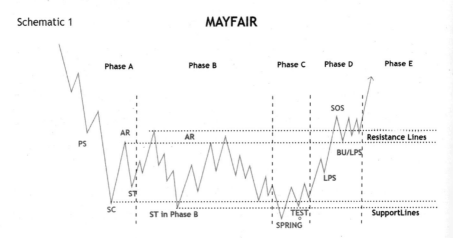

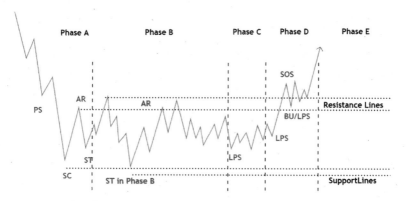

Schematic 2 — MAYFAIR

Moving from left to right, let's take a look at the key terms below:

PS: Preliminary Support. This will be the last major swing before the SC.

SC: Sellers' Climax. This, in theory, is the end of the down move for now, and a reaction is triggered as the key level is reached.

AR: Automatic Rally. After a sell-off (SC), the knee-jerk reaction causes a sharp move to the upside. It occurs without previous preparation, hence the word 'automatic'.

ST: Secondary Test. A name given by Wyckoff to the reaction following an automatic rally, where the price has another attempt at going down. If that test is associated with a small range and light volume, it increases the likelihood that the previous trend is over.

Spring: A form of a test of a trading range. Pushing prices below support by the strong hands to check the status of supply. The market's response to the spring indicates the nature of supply and demand forces for the near future.

Test: Much like the ST, this is the test of the spring. The last attempt to push the market lower. If support holds, then you can expect the move up to the upper half of the schematic.

LPS: Last Point of Support. A point at the end of the accumulation process where the strong hand operators (banks, funds, bigger traders) recognise that supply forces have exhausted themselves and it is safe to start marking up prices.

SOS: A Sign of Strength. A rally towards the top of the schematic. Ideally, this move will have a strong close and higher volume compared with the volume seen until now inside this range.

When drawing your schematic, you can draw a horizontal ray from the SC of the distribution. The next line will be at the AR; this gives you the rough range of the schematic. The next two horizontal rays will be at the points adjacent to the AR, both higher and lower swings. This gives a support and resistance range, as shown in the images above.

Although there are a lot of different terminologies associated with Wyckoff, such as creek jumps and breaking the ice, many are actually later editions added by students of Wyckoff. So, for the purpose of dumbing it down and keeping it simple, I will focus on what really matters when learning the basics.

After a lot of buying or selling, you expect a 'climax'. Then comes the profit-taking, which in the schematics are the ARs. From there, the accumulation and distribution can start all over again. The game is designed to fool retail traders in the wrong way, test the market confidence and collect more of the asset before marking it up or down (into the trend) – to the next climax. It's actual genius, and retail have fallen for this for decades!

'The stock market is a device for transferring money
from the impatient to the patient.'

Warren Buffett

## PHASES

In both accumulation and distribution schematics, you will notice
phases marked on the images.

### Accumulation Schematic Phases

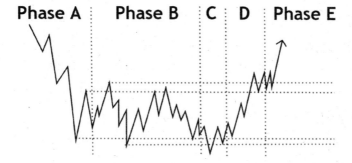

### Phase A

The selling force decreases, and the downtrend starts to slow
down. This phase is usually marked by an increase in trading
volume. The preliminary support (PS) indicates that some buyers
are showing up, but still not enough to stop the downward move.
The selling climax (SC) is formed by an intense selling activity as
investors capitulate. This is often a point of high volatility, where
panic selling creates big candlesticks and wicks.

The strong drop quickly reverts into a bounce or automatic
rally (AR) as buyers absorb the excessive supply. In general, the

trading range of an accumulation schematic is defined by the space between the SC low and the AR high.

As the name suggests, the secondary test (ST) happens when the market drops near the SC region, testing whether the downtrend is really over or not. At this point, the trading volume and market volatility tend to be lower. While the ST often forms a higher low in relation to the SC, that may not always be the case.

## Phase B

Based on Wyckoff's law of cause and effect, Phase B may be seen as the cause that leads to an effect. Essentially, Phase B is the consolidation stage, in which the Composite Man accumulates the highest number of assets. During this stage, the market tends to test both the resistance and support levels of the trading range. There may be numerous secondary tests (ST) during Phase B.

In some cases, they may produce higher highs (bull traps) and lower lows (bear traps) in relation to the SC and AR of Phase A.

## Phase C

A typical Accumulation Phase C contains what is called a spring. The spring often acts as the last bear trap before the market starts making higher lows. During Phase C, the Composite Man ensures that there is little supply left in the market (i.e. the traders that were going to sell already did). The spring often breaks the support levels to stop out opportunistic longs and help to mislead investors. It describes it as a final attempt to buy shares at a lower price before the uptrend starts. The bear trap induces retail investors to give up their holdings.

However, the support levels manage to hold in some cases, and the spring simply does not occur. In other words, there may be accumulation schematics that present all other elements but not the spring. Still, the overall scheme continues to be valid.

## Phase D

Phase D represents the transition between cause and effect. It stands between the accumulation zone (Phase C) and the breakout of the trading range (Phase E). Typically, Phase D shows a significant increase in trading volume and volatility. It usually has a last point support (LPS), making a higher low before the market moves higher. The LPS often precedes a breakout of the resistance levels, which in turn creates higher highs. This indicates signs of strength (SOS), as previous resistances become brand new supports. Despite the somewhat confusing terminology, there may be more than one LPS during Phase D. They often have increased trading volume while testing the new support lines. The price may create a small consolidation zone in some cases before effectively breaking the bigger trading range and moving to Phase E.

## Phase E

Phase E is the last stage of an accumulation schematic. It is marked by an evident breakout of the trading range caused by increased market demand. This is when the trading range is effectively broken and the uptrend starts.

# SHORTENING OF THE THRUST (SOT)

I mentioned the shortening of the thrust in the Elliott chapter, and it is also a useful concept while employing the Wyckoff method. Assessing the supply and demand characteristics of the market is critical, and the shortening of the thrust is a great way to spot trend reversals about to take place.

Another way to describe SOT is when you see a lot of effort (volume) and very little result in terms of price movement, causing the candles to contract and become smaller inside the channel.

In a rising or falling diagonal, the price might get tighter towards the end, hence the 'shortening of the thrust' towards that direction. When combining this insight with Elliott, Fibonacci or liquidity zones, you will quickly find that it's often a character trait for the price to slow in momentum as it nears an 'area of interest'.

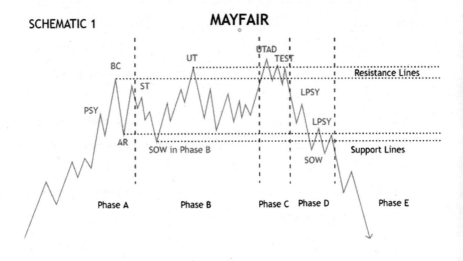

SCHEMATIC 1      **MAYFAIR**

## SCHEMATIC 2        MAYFAIR

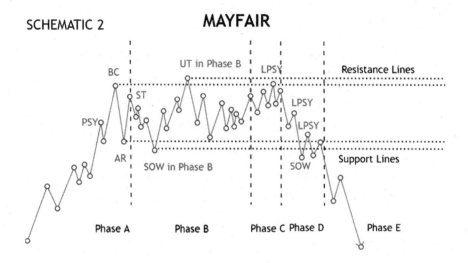

Again, let's go through these from left to right:

PSY: Preliminary Supply. The first significant reaction that occurs after a prolonged rally that indicates budding supply showing up. It is usually associated with a minor buying climax.

BC: Buying Climax. Major panic that occurs at the end of a steep ascent in prices. In its classical form, it is typified by a large range reversal in prices (big candles / wicks) accompanied by a large volume.

SOW: Sign of Weakness. A reaction during the process of distribution that is associated with a wide range, weak close and higher volumes.

UT: Upthrust. The mirror of a spring. It is a form of a test of a trading range, characterised by pushing prices above resistance.

Strong hands are checking the status of the demand. The market response to the upthrust indicates the nature of supply and demand forces for the near future.

UTAD: Upthrust After Distribution. A UTAD is the distributional counterpart to the spring and terminal shakeout in the accumulation schematic. It occurs in the latter stages of the schematic and provides a definitive test of new demand after a breakout above resistance.

LPSY: Last Point of Supply. A point at the end of the distribution process where the strong hands recognise that demand forces have exhausted themselves and it is safe to start marking down prices.

## DISTRIBUTION SCHEMATIC PHASES

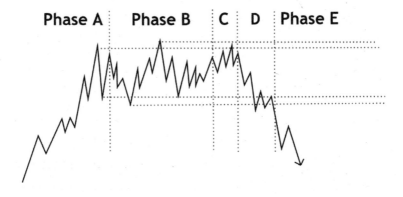

### Phase A

The first phase occurs when an established uptrend starts to slow down due to decreasing demand. The preliminary supply (PSY) suggests that the selling force is showing up, although still not strong enough to stop the upward movement. The buying climax (BC) is then formed by intense buying activity. This is usually caused by inexperienced traders that buy out of emotions. Perhaps they see a breakout of some kind.

Next, the strong move up causes an automatic reaction (AR) as the market makers absorb the excessive demand. In other words, the Composite Man starts distributing his holdings to the late buyers. The secondary test (ST) occurs when the market revisits the BC region, often forming a lower high.

## Phase B

Phase B of a distribution acts as the consolidation zone (cause) that precedes a downtrend (effect). During this phase, the Composite Man gradually sells his assets, absorbing and weakening market demand. Usually, the upper and lower bands of the trading range are tested multiple times, which may include short-term bear and bull traps. Sometimes, the market will move above the resistance level created by the BC, resulting in an ST that can also be called an upthrust (UT).

## Phase C

In some cases, the market will present one last bull trap after the consolidation period. It's called UTAD or upthrust after distribution. It is, basically, the opposite of an accumulation spring.

## Phase D

Phase D of a distribution is pretty much a mirror image of the Accumulation Phase D. It usually has a last point of supply (LPSY) in the middle of the range, creating a lower high. From this point, new LPSYs are created either around or below the support zone. An evident sign of weakness (SOW) appears when the market breaks below the support lines.

## Phase E

The last stage of a distribution marks the beginning of a downtrend, with an evident break below the trading range caused by a strong dominance of supply over demand.

**'MARKETS CAN STAY IRRATIONAL LONGER THAN YOU CAN STAY SOLVENT.'**
*JOHN MAYNARD KEYNES*

# Chapter 19

# GANN

Another emotional analyst – just like Elliott and Wyckoff – Gann is often considered one of the greats, and several of his techniques are still used in the markets today.

However, whilst Wyckoff and Elliott are mostly centred on the price action, Gann's techniques determine the time factors.

Some well-known Gann tools include:

1. Gann fans
2. Gann speed resistance fans
3. Gann boxes
4. Gann squares

In essence, they all have symmetry in common. They are all based on mathematics to do with market strength over time.

A Gann angle is a diagonal line that moves at a uniform rate of speed. It looks like a trend line but isn't placed in the same way. While a more traditional trend line is created by connecting bottoms to bottoms in the case of an uptrend, and tops to tops in the case of a downtrend, Gann angles are calculated using other price points.

The benefit of drawing a Gann angle compared to a trend line is that it allows the analyst to forecast where the price will be on a particular date in the future, as opposed to just where the price is going.

Gann angles cannot be considered perfect, nor will they necessarily predict the market point at a given time. They can help with assessing the strength and direction of the trend. Is it ahead or behind the Gann angle? Much like the simple trend line, the symmetry can become somewhat self-fulfilling.

## PAST, PRESENT AND FUTURE

The key concept to grasp when working with Gann angles is that the past, the present and the future are said to all exist at the same time on the angles. This helps forecast support and resistance levels, the strength of direction and the timing of tops and bottoms.

The market moves with symmetry. Elliott, Gann and Wyckoff all adopted the Dow Theory in one shape or another.

Here's a simple technique using Gann fans. Ignore how the angles are calculated for now. The intent is to frame the market in time and price, to give a matrix that can help track the trend.

Step 1. Zoom out and see the trend.

Here is the monthly time frame, and the assumption is an uptrend.

Step 2. Identify the major swing high and low.

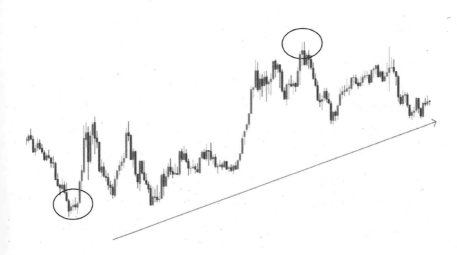

Step 3. Draw (with the magnet tool on) a horizontal line at the low of the low point and the high of the high point, followed by a vertical line on the point to the left. In this example, the left would be the low.

Step 4. Use the line angle tool (most charting platforms will have this) and go from both corners. From the bottom, draw a 45-degree angle, and from the top, draw a minus 45-degree angle.

Step 5. Anchor the Gann fan from the corner points and line up at 45-degree angles. Or, in the example below, the dashed line represents 50% of the rectangle. And where the two 45-degree points converge.

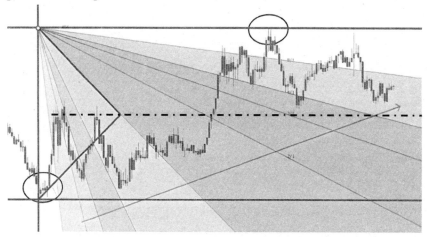

As you can see below, you can use the forecasted levels as part of your technical analysis with both fans applied. Whilst there are several other tools and techniques for Gann, the application will use a similar technique to add them to your charts.

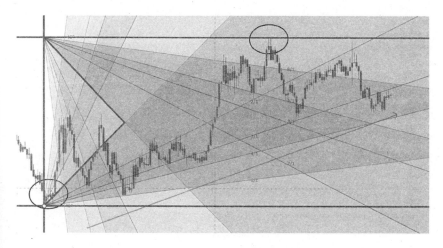

Using Gann angles to forecast support and resistance is probably the most popular way they are used. The technique frames the market, allowing the analyst to read the market's movement inside this framework. Uptrend angles provide the support, and downtrend angles provide the resistance.

Also, note how the market rotates from angle to angle. This is known as the 'rule of all angles'. This rule states that when the market breaks one angle, it will move towards the next one.

▼

Now, you might have read this chapter and thought to yourself, 'This seems a lot of effort. Why would I use this?' The truth is, you might not end up using it. So, why did I include it?

Many traders apply Gann – often wrongly – giving Gann a kind of self-fulfilling prophecy status. Ironically, Gann was an astrologer, so perhaps best you think of Gann's techniques a little like a horoscope.

However, it is not to be laughed at, so don't dismiss it just yet.

When building your strategy, you want to make most decisions as systematic as possible and thus easy to replicate.

When applying trend lines, the subjectivity can range with things like using three points or two. Do you use the highs and lows of candle bodies or their wicks?

However, when applying Gann levels, you can repeat the process time and time again, knowing 100% it will be the same every time. This is something worth keeping in mind when building the strategy.

Another visual technique I have found useful over the years is to take the Gann application, apply trend lines over the key levels, and then delete a lot of the noise. Here's my current version for Bitcoin in September 2021.

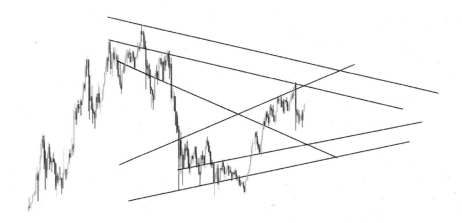

This makes it easier to see than keeping all of the fans on the chart.

'THE STOCK MARKET IS FILLED WITH INDIVIDUALS WHO KNOW THE PRICE OF EVERYTHING, BUT THE VALUE OF NOTHING.'
PHILIP ARTHUR FISHER

## Chapter 20

# EXAMPLE SCENARIO

After finishing a book, I am aware that you are often left wondering, 'Now what?' I wanted to add a scenario section to give a real-world example of where these teachings can be used, how to spot them on a chart, and a step-by-step example of the logic.

## PUTTING IT ALL TOGETHER

You need to first look at a longer time frame, and below is the monthly chart.

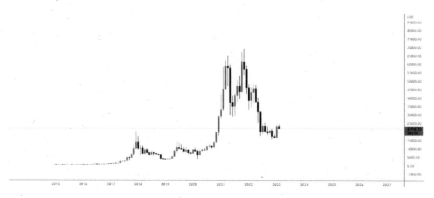

What you are looking for to begin with is the general trend direction. This is a tricky one on this particular chart, but you have a very large uptrend and a slightly smaller downtrend. Can you see them?

The analysis will always be subjective, so what you now need to do is look for the logic that will provide a stronger bias.

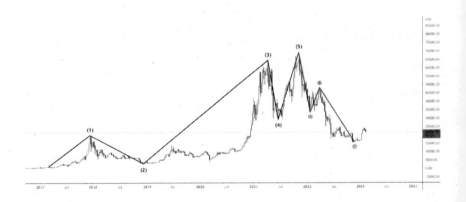

I have counted the five waves up and currently we are seeing three waves down, marked A, B and C.

## EXAMPLE SCENARIO

I will now add the Weiss Wave indicator to the chart.

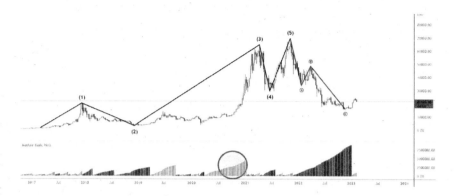

This has instantly confirmed the count being 3 the largest and of course the large red wave on the far right suggests the down move 'might' be over.

From here, I feel somewhat confident that we have had a good enough move from the 5 high position to the downside. I also like the view that A to B marked in orange was a redistribution. If you remember the Wyckoff phases – we should now be entering Accumulation on a very long time frame.

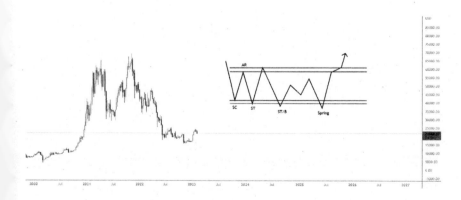

What I've done here, is put a 'rough' schematic, the reason I have done this is to highlight that you won't always see a textbook example. What I am trying to identify here on the chart is some basic concepts.

In doing so, I have found potentially two options – again, before you look below can you spot one or both options?

Option 1: could the low followed by a little rally be the SC and AR?

Here is Option 2:

## EXAMPLE SCENARIO

This option has a more likely candidate for the AR. Remember what causes an AR? The AR stands for Automatic Rally (or reaction from a buyer's climax), a rally that occurs after a Selling Climax. It occurs without previous preparation, hence the word 'automatic'.

In both scenarios we are likely early in an accumulation schematic of a very long time-frame move.

With that in mind, now zoom out even further. If a 0–5 move gives us the current all-time high (ATH), then what if this was the first major cycle and the 5 was the (1) of a much larger move. We are now seeing the A, B, C of the larger degree (2).

From here, what you want to look for now is more evidence of the move away from the 2 above. If we draw Fibonacci levels from the 0 to the current all-time high at $69,000, we can see we have hit a 0.618 retracement and the next key level 0.786 (78.6%) is at $14,766.

All of which is acceptable and plausible for this viewpoint.

To summarise: we could be at a 2 of a substantial wave degree.

We are looking for signs of Accumulation inside a Wyckoff schematic. See the COT chart below:

This would suggest with the long positions rising, another piece of evidence hinting towards Accumulation.

You see how you can build a story and back it up with logic. These techniques can be used on any type of chart. Within reason, if you are trying to analyse some unknown altcoin with a week's worth of chart data, you will be hard pushed.

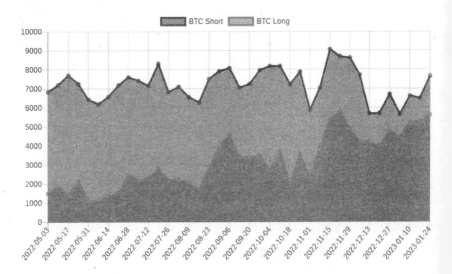

# 'IN INVESTING WHAT IS COMFORTABLE IS RARELY PROFITABLE.'

## ROBERT ARNOTT

'SUCCESSFUL INVESTING TAKES TIME, DISCIPLINE AND PATIENCE.'

WARREN BUFFETT

## Chapter 21

# CONCLUSION

I want to thank you for taking the time to read this book.

When I started writing, it was with the story of the 'turtle traders' in mind. If you haven't read it, it's from a brilliant book by Michael Covel, called *The Complete Turtle Trader*. The story is about two partners who have a little wager about whether anyone can be taught to trade.

In writing this book, I strongly feel that it can be done, and I think *Master the Art of Trading* can help any trader, new or established. All it takes is a little patience and some simple steps.

Over my 20 plus years of trading and endless reading of trading books, I have studied various techniques – some of which worked, some of which did not. What I found interesting was that you have experts in the field much like with any other topic. Each practitioner will give their opinion; the issue is that it's often one-sided. I know Elliott Wave traders, day traders, scalpers, traders who only focus on Wyckoff and others who specialise in algorithmic trading. The majority of trading books have a niche or a focus on primarily one aspect of trading.

So, my logic for this book was all about condensing years of experience and knowledge from countless books into one simple-to-follow, methodical format.

So please forgive me for glossing over some of the things I didn't see as relevant. Each of the covered topics has a lot more depth, which you can go into if you choose. For me personally, the 90% I left out was not important enough. Any more detail than what I have included in this book could easily run the risk of over-complicating things.

Dow, Elliott, Wyckoff and Gann showed their understanding beyond just technical analysis. They understood how human emotions fit on to charts, creating patterns that can be deciphered.

It makes sense that until humans change their psychology, the methods of such great masters will remain profitable.

Unlike other books that focus on a tunnelled vision view of one element of technical analysis, this book intended to interlock all the great masters' emotional understanding with a methodical process that can be replicated time and time again.

I hope you have enjoyed reading this. You are also welcome to join us on the Mayfair Method server. A like-minded community awaits, where I would be happy to answer your questions and go into depth on the topics within the book.

# CONCLUSION

**What people say about the Mayfair Method**

'I'm excited. It's like seeing the matrix for the first time – finding patterns in chaos.'

'This is the best write-up on crypto and alt coins I have ever come across.'

'You helped me save more than GEICO ever could.'

'Thanks for the helpful tutorial on Gann. We hope it helps others learn something new. It's been featured in Editors' Picks.'

'A life-changing phone call, now starting to see the bigger picture.'

'I'm accusing Lewis of being the Composite Man.'

'I found an expert with experience.'

'Thanks for selling shovels during the gold rush.'

'I want to be like you one day . . . a HERO.'

'I thought Lewis was a sophisticated AI Bot, too good.'

'It's been a privilege to learn from the Mayfair Group. They have given next-level content and insane tools.'

'Yeah, the Composite Man put gremlins in Lewis's computer. They can't let him share all the secrets.'

'Talk about gold, surprisingly, Lewis was right again ;-)'

'In a nutshell, you covered all my questions. Ten years of learning, and you matched it in an hour.'

'Being a psychiatric nurse, I can completely give you a professional opinion and say to you, you are exactly correct on your "Understanding the Traders' Psychology" diagram. That is very comparable to the 5 Stages of Grief and Dying, also known as the 5 Stages of Death.'

'This is the most intelligent analysis I have ever read.'

'You do realise that the book recommendations and your guidance have changed my life.'

'This man is the best analyst on TradingView.'

'One question for Lewis, well two actually:
   1. Are you the composite operator?
   2. If not, do you know him & have daily contact?'

'Lewis said in 5 minutes what some guy on YouTube took an hour and a half to try and break down.'

'I feel so lucky to have found this awesome gem of a trader.'

'I guess Lewis knows his shit.'

'It pains me to admit it, but you were 100% right.'

'Like there's a spy among us, Mayfair really is a master of puppets.'

'Good one, like the proverb: Today you are dripping honey.'

'Wow, so cool, Mayfair just commented on my post – I must be right.'

'You're more than an expert.'

'I am sure I speak for many when I say you are "must-read" content.'

'You called this to a T so far, how, just how?'

'I just copied your style. Thanks for the publications. Changed my whole business model.'

'I have listened to Lewis's last stream at least three times. How can I download them?'

'Near perfect, the bit that wasn't was my own mistake. Thanks for everything.'

'It's a mental game training for me, not just in trading. It's helped me in everyday life as well.'

'Learning from the best.'

# ACKNOWLEDGEMENTS

If someone had told me a year ago that I'd become a published author I would have laughed – but here we are!

It wouldn't have become a reality if it weren't for the following people:

My history teacher for wangling a trip to New York that begun my trading journey.

My bank manager for learning how to execute a trade, as I'm sure I was the first ever trader at the local branch.

My father for reminding me why people should learn how to trade.

My current trading partner Paul, for making me feel young, as he is a bit old. But, in all fairness, he's a good sounding-board and we've had some great times educating a brilliant crowd.

On that note, I want to thank my Discord members for their continuous support of the Mayfair Method. It's their testimonials and desire to learn that keeps me wanting to help all the more.

I'd like to thank my good friend Dee for his support and contacts list, as well as his friendship throughout the years. And I also want to thank Surry, who knew the right person to put my manuscript in front of.

Then, in terms of creating this book:

I'd like to thank my son Zack for his endless cups of tea and help with my spelling, punctuation, and grammar.

I'd like to thank Rik, my editor, for his support and guidance throughout the whole process.

I'd also like to thank my wife for help with these acknowledgments, amongst other things! But most of all I want to thank her for being so incredible. She really is my everything.

Finally, I'd like to thank you for reading my book. I hope it helps you on your trading journey.

Feel free to contact me via email at welshexpertgeneralist@gmail.com.

And, of course, come join our Discord community: https://discord.gg/5t3w47raHe!

# GLOSSARY

**Bollinger Band:** A Bollinger Band ® is a technical analysis tool defined by a set of trend lines. They are plotted as two standard deviations, both positively and negatively, away from a simple moving average (SMA) of a security's price and can be adjusted to user preferences.

\* Sourced https://www.investopedia.com/terms/b/bollingerbands.asp

**Day Trader:** exactly as it says on the tin – these traders will look to open and close positions in a day. Not always, but likely. Unlike a scalper, the number of positions will be less. You will also see and hear of these traders as intraday traders.

**Death Cross:** The death cross is a market chart pattern reflecting recent price weakness. It refers to the drop of a short-term moving average – meaning the average of recent closing prices for a stock, stock index, commodity or cryptocurrency over a set period of time – below a longer-term moving average. The most closely watched stock market moving averages are the 50-day and the 200-day.

**Intraday Traders**: see Day Trader.

**MACD:** Moving average convergence/divergence (MACD, or MAC-D) is a trend-following momentum indicator that shows the relationship between two exponential moving averages (EMAs) of a security's price. The MACD line is calculated by subtracting the 26-period EMA from the 12-period EMA.
* Sourced https://www.investopedia.com/terms/m/macd.asp

**Moving Average:** In finance, a moving average (MA) is a stock indicator commonly used in technical analysis. The reason for calculating the moving average of a stock is to help smooth out the price data by creating a constantly updated average price.

By calculating the moving average, the impacts of random, short-term fluctuations on the price of a stock over a specified time frame are mitigated. Simple moving averages (SMAs) use a simple arithmetic average of prices over some time span, while exponential moving averages (EMAs) place greater weight on more recent prices than older ones over the time period.
* Sourced https://www.investopedia.com/terms/m/
movingaverage.asp

**P&L:** Profit and loss or P&L is the average profit compared to the loss of a trade. You will see references of 3:1 as an example so for every $300 profit, you would be willing to risk $100. This simply means if a trade goes to plan you make 300 and if it goes wrong the exposure was 100.

# GLOSSARY

**Pip:** 'Pip' is short for percentage in point or price interest point. The 'pip' is the smallest whole unit price move that an exchange rate can make, based on forex market convention.

**Rollover:** In the forex market, there is what's known as rollover. This is the process of extending the settlement date of an open position. In most currency trades, a trader is required to take delivery of the currency two days after the transaction date. Which simply means one bank wants delivery and the other wants payment.

**RSI:** The relative strength index (RSI) is a momentum indicator used in technical analysis. RSI measures the speed and magnitude of a security's recent price changes to evaluate overvalued or undervalued conditions in the price of that security.

The RSI is displayed as an oscillator (a line graph) on a scale of zero to 100. The indicator was developed by J. Welles Wilder Jr. and introduced in his seminal 1978 book, *New Concepts in Technical Trading Systems*.
* Sourced https://www.investopedia.com/terms/r/rsi.asp

**Scalping:** a style used by traders which simply means buying or selling with a brief hold time. The idea is to profit from very small movements in the price action. This would also likely mean a scalper will make a large number of trades throughout the day, week and month.

**Sentiment:** Market sentiment represents how a group feels about the market or economy.

**Stochastic:** A stochastic oscillator is a momentum indicator comparing a particular closing price of a security to a range of its prices over a certain period of time. The sensitivity of the oscillator to market movements is reducible by adjusting that time period or by taking a moving average of the result. It is used to generate overbought and oversold trading signals, utilising a 0–100 bounded range of values.
* Sourced https://www.investopedia.com/terms/s/stochastico-scillator.asp

**Swing Traders:** can be described as a type of trading method in which positions are held for longer than a single day. Starting with scalpers who are in and out quickly, day traders or intraday who hold for usually one day or less, swing traders are traders who hold a position for several days. You could add one other style of trader above this – this we would call investor. Investors trade for weeks and months on end, sometimes years.

# NOTES

7    Henry Ford quote sourced from Books That Can Change Your Life, at: https://books-that-can-change-your-life.net/best-quotes-from-henry-ford

23    Nicolas Darvas quote sourced from Day Trade the World at: https://www.daytradetheworld.com/trading-blog/analyze-avoid-forecasting

26    Bill Lipschutz quote sourced from Daily Price Action at: https://dailypriceaction.com/blog/bill-lipschutz

28    Larry Hite quote sourced from The Cite Site at: https://thecitesite.com/authors/larry-hite

30    Alexander Elder quote sourced from Quote Fancy at: https://quotefancy.com/quote/1791105/Alexander-Elder-The-goal-of-a-successful-trader-is-to-make-the-best-trades-Money-is

30    Yvan Byeajee quote sourced from Goodreads at: https://www.goodreads.com/quotes/8989612-confidence-is-not-i-will-profit-on-this-trade-confidence

31    Jack Schwager quote sourced from Hugo's Way at: https://hugosway.com/amateurs-think-about-how-much-money-they-can-make-professionals-think-about-how-much-money-they-could-lose-jack-schwager/

41    Malcolm Muggeridge quote sourced from Goodreads at: https://www.goodreads.com/quotes/726614-all-new-news-is-old-news-happening-to-new-people

47    Sir John Templeton quote sourced from Seeking Alpha at: https://seekingalpha.com/article/4573513-bull-markets-are-born-on-pessimism

53    The Companies House web portal can be visited at: https://www.gov.uk/get-information-about-a-company

57    Peter Lynch quote sourced from Brainy Quote at: https://www.brainyquote.com/authors/peter-lynch-quotes

61    Mark Cuban quote reported by Horsch, AJ, Mark Cuban: 'Everyone is a genius in a bull market', CNBC: 2020; available at: https://www.cnbc.com/2020/07/20/mark-cuban-everybody-is-a-genius-in-a-bull-market.html

77    Yvan Byeajee quote sourced from Goodreads at: https://www.goodreads.com/quotes/8989641-the-mind-is-a-fascinating-instrument-that-can-make-or

# NOTES

85   This definition of Dow Theory is influenced from
     Wikipedia at: https://en.wikipedia.org/wiki/Dow_theory

86   Bernard Baruch quote reported by Nagar, Anupam,
     'Investing gems from Bernard Baruch', *Economic Times*,
     2023; available at: https://economictimes.indiatimes.com/
     markets/stocks/news/stock-market-tries-to-make-a-fool-
     of-you-and-how-investing-gems-from-bernard-baruch/
     articleshow/79460869

87   Ralph Seger quote is sourced from Quotery
     at: https://www.quotery.com/quotes/
     investor-without-investment-objectives-like

89   Richard Wyckoff quote reported by Nagar, Anupam,
     'Richard Wyckoff's tips to study market trends
     for super stock selection', Economic Times, 2022;
     available at: https://economictimes.indiatimes.
     com/markets/stocks/news/richard-wyckoffs-tips-
     to-study-market-trends-for-super-stock-selection/
     articleshow/91026458

93   Jesse Livermore quote sourced from Hugo's Way at:
     https://hugosway.com/do-not-anticipate-and-move-with-
     out-market-confirmation-being-a-little-late-in-your-
     trade-is-your-insurance-that-you-are-right-or-wrong-jes-
     se-livermore/

98   Nison, Steve. *Japanese Candlestick Charting Techniques: A
     Contemporary Guide to the Ancient Investment Techniques of
     the Far East*, 2nd Edition (Pearson, 2001)

105   George Soros   quote sourced from AZ Quotes at: https://
www.azquotes.com/quote/527424

125   Thomas Jefferson quote sourced from Goodreads at:
https://www.goodreads.com/quotes/1361034-if-you-want-
something-you-ve-never-had-you-must-be

126   Doug Gregory quote sourced from Hugo's Way at https://
hugosway.com/trade-whats-happening-not-what-you-
think-is-gonna-happen-doug-gregory

133   William Feather quote sourced from Brainy
Quote at: https://www.brainyquote.com/quotes/
william_feather_391335

151   Charlie Munger quote sourced from Quote Fancy at:
https://quotefancy.com/quote/756828/Charlie-Munger-
The-big-money-is-not-in-the-buying-and-selling-but-in-
the-waiting

158   Seth Klarman quote sourced from AZ Quotes at:
https://www.azquotes.com/quote/1407218

159   Eves, Howard. *An Introduction to the History of Mathematics*
(Brooks Cole, 1990). p. 261

163   Hemant Beniwal quote sourced from
Fortune at: https://fortune.com/2012/07/30/
most-dangerous-words-in-finance-this-time-its-different/

168   Yvan Byeajee quote sourced from Sloan, Allan, 'Most
dangerous words in finance: "This time it's different"',

Fortune: 2012; available at: https://www.goodreads.com/author/quotes/13726354.Yvan_Byeajee

183   Jesse Livermore quote sourced from Quote Fancy at: https://quotefancy.com/quote/1639521/Jesse-Lauriston-Livermore-There-is-time-to-go-long-time-to-go-short-and-time-to-go

186   Paul Samuelson quote sourced from Brainy Quote at: https://www.brainyquote.com/quotes/paul_samuelson_205549

189   Warren Buffett quote sourced from Reese, John, 'Winning in the market with the patience of the Wright brothers and Warren Buffett', Forbes: 2018; available at: https://www.forbes.com/sites/investor/2018/01/30/winning-in-the-market-with-the-patience-of-the-wright-brothers-and-warren-buffett

199   John Maynard Keynes quote sourced from Wild, Royston, 'How to pick stocks: finding companies to invest in', The Motley Fool: 2023; available at: https://www.fool.co.uk/investing-basics/how-to-invest-in-shares/finding-companies-to-invest-in

209   Philip Arthur quote sourced from AZ Quotes at: https://www.azquotes.com/quote/527417

219   Robert Arnott quote sourced from Goodreads at: https://www.goodreads.com/quotes/10266897-in-investing-what-is-comfortable-is-rarely-profitable

220 Warren Buffett quote sourced from AZ Quote at: https://www.azquotes.com/quote/689441